G. Dallas Lind

Methods of Teaching in Country Schools

G. Dallas Lind

Methods of Teaching in Country Schools

ISBN/EAN: 9783337427542

Printed in Europe, USA, Canada, Australia, Japan

Cover: Foto ©Paul-Georg Meister /pixelio.de

More available books at **www.hansebooks.com**

IN

COUNTRY SCHOOLS.

BY

G. DALLAS LIND.

DANVILLE, INDIANA:
THE "NORMAL TEACHER" PUBLISHING HOUSE,
J. E. SHERRILL, PROPRIETOR.
CHAS. L. WOLFE, PRINTER.
1880.

Entered according to Act of Congress, in the year 1879, by
J. E. SHERRILL,
In the office of the Librarian of Congress at Washington.
ALL RIGHTS RESERVED.

DEDICATION.

To THE teachers of the country schools of the U. S., those who stand nominally on the lowest round of the Educational ladder, yet who possess the power to wield the greatest influence on the civilization and culture of our people, this volume is respectfully dedicated.

PREFACE.

THIS book was written for country teachers, by a country teacher and though doubtless full of imperfections, it is hoped by the author that many things which he has learned in the school of experience, that dearest of teachers, the reader may learn by a careful perusal of its contents.

Captious critics may find much to worry over, but the writer can assure them that they will not find anything which he has not worried over before them.

A strictly logical arrangement of the subject has not been attempted. It was thought that a familiar conversational style was better adapted to the purpose in hand.

It will be observed that frequent references are made from one part of the book to another. This was done to avoid repetition, and it is hoped the teachers will make use of them.

Central Normal College, Danville, Ind.

TABLE OF CONTENTS.

PART I.—SCHOOL MANAGEMENT.

CHAPTER I.—THE TEACHER.

SEC. 1.—Moral Qualifications	9
SEC. 2.—Mental Qualifications	10
SEC. 3.—Physical Qualifications	14
SEC. 4.—Literary and Scientific Qualifications	18
SEC. 5.—Spirit of the Teacher	23
SEC. 6.—Personal Habits	25
SEC. 7.—In Relation to Patrons	27
SEC. 8.—In Relation to Society	31
SEC. 9.—In Relation to the Profession	31

CHAPTER II.—THE SCHOOL.

SEC. 1.—Preliminary Work	34
SEC. 2.—Organizing	37
SEC. 3.—Conducting Recitations	39
SEC. 4.—Government	44

CHAPTER III.—THE SCHOOL-HOUSE.

SEC. 1.—School Architecture	55
SEC. 2.—School Apparatus	62
SEC. 3.—Ventilation	64

PART II.—METHODS OF TEACHING.

CHAP. I.—Reading - - - - - - 68
CHAP. II.—Spelling and Defining - - - 88
CHAP. III.—Arithmetic - - - - - 99
CHAP. IV.—Geography - - - - - 113
CHAP. V.—Grammar - - - - - 127
CHAP. VI.—History - - - - - 142
CHAP. VII.—Anatomy, Physiology and Hygiene - 149
CHAP. VIII.—Algebra and the Higher Mathematics 155
CHAP. IX.—Natural Sciences - - - - 159
CHAP. X.—Morals and Manners - - - 169
CHAP. XI.—Model Recitations - - - - 183
CHAP. XII.—Miscellaneous - - - - 199
CHAP. XIII.—Hints and Helps for the Teacher - 216

PART I--SCHOOL MANAGEMENT.

CHAPTER I.

THE TEACHER.

I. MORAL QUALIFICATIONS.

ALL men, even the most vicious, will admit that he who is immoral should not be placed in the position of teacher of youth. Popular opinion says teachers should have a good moral character, and all certificates require it, but how often, alas, is there a failure in carrying out this provision in practice. A man may be a very immoral man and yet find no trouble in getting some one or more persons to certify to his moral character. The law can not reach this matter except in cases of out-breaking immorality. It rests, then, with the teacher himself and with his conscience. Ask yourself, young man, if you are a fit person to enter that sacred temple. Pause and purify yourself on the threshhold. Remember that you carry about you a moral or immoral atmosphere according to the condition of the soul within, and that the innocent youth must imbibe that atmosphere be it healthful or poisonous. It is impossible for any one to be a successful hypocrite. He may be morally rotten at heart and attempt to make an outward show of morality for the purpose of obtaining and holding his position as teacher, but youth are not so easily deceived and moral instruction will have but little weight coming from such a man. The inward character of a man will crop out in spite of himself. In his teaching, in his government, in his conversation, in the family, or on the play ground, the character of the teacher will exhibit itself unconsciously to him but plainly to others. Says Dr. Holland, "The mind that has become a treasure house of truth and beauty speaks a world into existence with every utterance. * * * We give what we have received—that which is in us will out of us. Expression is the necessity of possession." If the teacher's heart is a "treasure house of truth and beauty" it will overflow, exerting an ennobling influence on all who may come near it. On the other hand if it be a "whitened sepulcher, filled with dead men's bones and all uncleanness," it will pollute all who have to deal with it.

The teacher must be not only a moral but a religious man, not of that kind who love to "display to congregations wide, devotions, every grace except the heart," but one who loves God and his fellow man and obeys the golden rule, not from policy but as the deep seated conviction of his soul.

II. MENTAL QUALIFICATIONS.

The teacher may be a truly moral and religious man and yet be entirely incompetent. He must have certain mental qualifications. It is not my purpose here to enter into a lengthy discussion of the mental faculties of man, but simply to hint at a few things by which the teacher may measure himself.

1. *He should have a cheerful and hopeful disposition.* The school-room is no place for a gloomy, sour, despondent nature. Children and youth are naturally buoyant and hopeful, but their impressible natures may be easily warped by constant contact with a morose disposition.

2. *He should be kind and benevolent.* No human heart is proof against the power of kindness. Even brute nature may be greatly impressed by it. I need not enlarge upon this point, although it would be easy to multiply words. The reader can see for himself the necessity of this faculty in a teacher.

3. *He should be open, frank and unsuspicious.* These are noble qualities, but I would not be misunderstood here. I do not mean that a teacher should be so unsuspicious that he will consider all children as born angels who can do no harm. Children sometimes need watching, but the teacher who acts as a detective or spy and constantly exhibits that disposition should have no place in the school-room. He should ever remember that there is a spark of honor in every breast and that sentiment should be appealed to and trusted in if he would attain control over vicious dispositions. He should always be ready to confess himself in the wrong when he sees he has made a mistake.

4. *He should have a love of the work.* This implies a love for children. He who has not the faculty called by Phrenologists Philoprogenitiveness well developed, should not choose the profession of teacher. He must have a love for the profession or he can not take a deep

interest in it. He can have little control of children unless he can sympathize with them and he can not sympathize with them unless he loves them. He should have this love sufficiently strong to be able to encourage their efforts and bear with their shortcomings, to feel for their sorrows, to lift up the despondent, to bring out the timid, to hold in check the bold, to conquer the obstinate and in general to throw his whole soul into the work of improving their physical, mental and moral condition.

5. *He should be conscientious.* This faculty leads a man to do right because it is right; to shun the wrong because it is wrong. He must feel that it is his duty to teach well and feel conscience-smitten if he leaves undone what he might have done for the benefit of those under his care. Without this feeling no one can become a good teacher. All men have this faculty in some degree, but those in whom it is feebly developed are the rogues, scoundrels and hypocrites of society. A lack of this feeling has filled our jails and penitentiaries and furnished subjects for the gallows. This faculty should be cultivated in children and youth, and the teacher who has it largely developed himself is best calculated to teach it.

6. *He should be a lover of order.* In no place is order and system needed more than in the school-room. If the teacher be not naturally systematic, he should use his utmost endeavors to improve himself in this respect. Let him make order and system a study. Let him practice it everywhere, even to the minor details of daily duties. He should practice keeping the articles in his room in order, the books on the shelves, &c., until it becomes a kind of second nature to him.

7. *He should be firm and self-reliant.* This quality

may easily be carried to extremes. Many men have the faculty of firmness so well developed that it becomes mere obstinacy and mulishness, or they are so impressed with the importance of being sole master of whatever is in their charge that they become tyrants and despots. The true teacher must avoid either extreme. If he is kind and conscientious and loves children he can be firm without being despotic, self-reliant without being bigoted and can govern with justice and equity.

8. *He should have a social and agreeable nature.* A teacher should have none of the disposition of a hermit. He may succeed in some other occupations and not be of a social nature, but in this he can not. The teacher's business is to improve society and therefore he must make himself one of the mass. He must have a kind word for every one, must have the power of adapting himself to different classes of people and making his company agreeable to them, but at the same time maintaining his self-respect and moral dignity. (See pp. 29 and 31).

To be a good teacher a man should have a good brain, all the mental faculties well developed. A man may be able to make a good wagon wheel or pair of boots and be greatly lacking in many of the mental faculties. He may be a good penman, musician, or artist, and lack conscientiousness and benevolence. But a man can not be a successful teacher who is greatly lacking in any faculty, that is he can not teach everything. The teacher in our public schools is required to teach something of almost everything, either directly or indirectly. Such also is the intimate inter-relation of the branches of knowledge that to be proficient in any one branch a man must have some acquaintance with all other branches. A man can not teach that which he does not know. A teacher can not have too much knowledge. He can not have a knowledge of a branch unless he has a good development of the mental faculty which is necessary to have, in order to acquire that branch. (See p. 18).

Do not think, teacher, that it is absolutely necessary to be born with a full development of these mental qualifications. Almost any person of ordinary mental calibre can acquire these qualifications by persistent study and practice. If, then, you are lacking in some of the mental faculties necessary to make a good teacher let it be your constant study to improve yourself. Let the motto, "KNOW THYSELF," be ever present before your mind, and apply your energies to the improvement of those parts which are lacking. You may be lacking in one faculty and yet be able to make up for it in part by a full development of some other faculty, but nothing is of so great advantage as a brain well balanced. If you are greatly lacking in any of these parts you would better seek some other employment as the experience necessary to improve you will be at the expense of your pupils and patrons and a constant source of vexation to yourself. If every teacher would look in upon himself and when he finds he is not fitted for the place he occupies, would step down and out and enter some other profession or adopt some other employment, the condition of our schools would soon improve rapidly.

III. PHYSICAL QUALIFICATIONS.

The teacher must have good health. The school-room is not a proper place for an invalid. It is often the case, that persons who are from some physical defect unfitted for occupations requiring manual labor, enter the teaching profession, hoping thus to make a living. Again, many enter the profession with good constitutions to retire from it in a few years with impaired health and seek some other occupation from which they hope to regain their lost vitality. The former should not and the latter need not be the case. No man who from physical reasons is unable to work should make this an excuse for teaching school. If he has the proper mental qualifications and good health, though he may lack a limb or the use of one, yet he is capable of teaching school. If the teacher understands and practices the laws of health, he may live as long and enjoy as good health as in any other occupation. There is not space in a treatise of this kind for a full discussion of the question of hygiene. A few hints and suggestions, however, will not be out of place.

A man may follow some out-door occupation, being possessed of a robust constitution, and live and enjoy excellent health for years and never take a thought about the matter. Exercise of the body, pure air and sunshine will go far towards making up for excesses in eating and drinking, or for want of sleep. But a teacher is for a great part of the time deprived of the opportunity for bodily exercise, often of pure air and sunshine. He should then whenever opportunity presents take daily exercise in the open air and sunshine. Most country teachers board or live at some distance from the school-house and the necessary walk to and from school affords an opportunity to enjoy these three essentials of health. Some persons need more exercise than others. Those of a rough and sturdy build need bodily exercise more than those of more delicate frame. Persons with delicate frames often overdo this matter of exercise and the very thing which, if properly conducted would be of great benefit, becomes an injury to them. Exercise to be beneficial should stop short of moderate fatigue.

The teacher should not be above manual labor. An hour each day spent in chopping or sawing wood would, in many cases, be of great benefit to the teacher's health and would not detract from his popularity. Let the teacher take his place on the play ground and exercise with the pupils in their games. (See 228.) The study of some branch of Natural Science, as Botany, Zoology, or Geology, will necessarily lead the teacher to take walks in pursuit of knowledge. Such rambles among rocks and trees will be food for both body and mind. Riding on horseback, rowing, skating, driving, working in the garden, or at the various occupations on the farm are all to be highly recommended, if not indulged in to excess, as beneficial to the teacher's health.

What must I say about diet? Books have been written on the subject and yet men may follow their instructions to the letter and come out in a few years dyspeptics. But I will say, be temperate. It is not so much what you eat as it is how you eat it. Regular meals when the occupation is regular, and moderate in quantity, eaten slowly, with cheerful company, not too great a variety at one meal to tempt the appetite, but a variety from day to day, not very much animal food, an avoidance of pastry, plenty of ripe fruits and vegetables, food coarse rather than fine—these requirements will keep one in health so far as diet is concerned.

Another essential to perfect health is cleanliness. Frequent bathing of the whole body in warm or tepid water with free use of soap and frequent change of underclothing will go far towards maintaining health. Bathing may be carried to excess. The skin may be excited unduly, causing extreme sensitiveness to changes of temperature. Once a week in winter, and two or three times a week in summer is often enough. The same clothing that is worn in day time, should not be worn at night. The clothes worn next the skin in day time should be removed, and allowed to air at night. They may be put on again in the morning, and those worn at night allowed to air.

Tobacco, tea, coffee and spirituous liquors, are not necessary for any one, and though not all of them always injurious, the teacher will do well to let them severely alone. (See p. 25).

I have given here a few hints which I trust will be regarded by the teacher, and if he is not already informed in the matter of hygiene, I hope he will study it, and apply his knowledge to the care of his physical organization.

Said John Locke, nearly two hundred years ago, "A sound mind in a sound body is a short, but full description of a happy state in this world." A man can not have a perfectly sound mind without a sound body, and certainly, though one may enjoy existence without a sound mind, he is not capable of filling the position of teacher.

2

IV. SCIENTIFIC AND LITERARY QUALIFICATIONS.

It is generally supposed that to teach a primary school or such a school as is generally found in country districts, requires but slight culture and scholarship. While it is true that a man may be a good and successful teacher of the common branches, and know nothing whatever of Latin or Greek, or of the higher mathematics, or of the natural sciences, it is also true, that had he knowledge of these higher branches, he would be a better teacher. To say nothing of the culture and enlargement of the mind, by the study of science, and languages, the mere knowledge obtained is of great value, even to the teacher of the most primary class.

Under the present state of society, we can not expect teachers all to be great scholars. They may commence teaching with no more education than that to be obtained in common country schools, but they should not be content with that. While they teach they should study, study not only how best to teach, but to improve their minds in higher branches of knowledge. (See page 13).

The teacher should always be a learner, and if he is a true teacher, he will learn more than his pupils. He will learn not only more of the branches he is teaching, but will make rapid progress in the higher branches of knowledge. His first endeavor should be to attain ordinary proficiency in the branches he is required to teach. This he should have before attempting to manage a school. Then while teaching he should study the lessons ahead of his classes, that he may come before them prepared to demonstrate any point which may come up.

At the same time he is keeping ahead of his classes in the common branches, he should pursue some one of the higher branches. He should not, however, undertake too many studies at once. Let him take one extra study at a time, and when he has attained considerable proficiency, take up another.

Many a young man has acquired a knowledge of the higher branches by study of books without a teacher, and many young men can yet do so, but in these days of cheap schools, no young man who expects to become a teacher, should fail to spend at least one term in some Normal school, or institution where he may obtain a knowledge of literature and science. He may, if he have a good common school education, teach a term or two in the country and then spend his earnings in taking a course of study in some wide-awake institution. I would not recommend a college course, where the energetic country youth is held back to keep pace with sons of rich men, who are sent there to spend their fathers' money, and receive a thin coat of polish which will not stand the hard knocks of that greatest educator of all, the actual business world. The young man may do as I have known young men to do, borrow money to take a course at school, and then go home and teach, and earn the money to pay it back. If such a course can be pursued, the young man can well afford to pay a good interest on the money.

You can acquire the fundamental principles of the sciences under a competent instructor, and in contact with others who are enthusiastically pursuing the same study, much more rapidly than by your own unaided study. Having thus had a start, you can pursue these branches at your leisure, during your odd moments, and while you are earning some money, and improving yourself in the common branches, and in the art of teaching school, and gaining experience of great value.

Much may be learned by improving the odd moments. It is said that Dickens never wrote more than two hours a day, and we wonder at the immense amount of literary work he accomplished. But a short time each day will accomplish wonders. It is not the protracted efforts once in a month or so that count, but it is the little every day. Let no day pass in which you do not do some studying, be it ever so little. The teacher has ample time if he improve it properly, to inform himself. He has mornings and evenings and Saturdays to study. He can also use a portion of his noons and recesses in looking over his lessons for the day.

It is best to have some regular programme for study and recreation. For example, let him devote half an hour each morning and evening to the study of some science, not allowing any ordinary circumstances to detract from this half-hour twice each day. Let him devote an hour each Saturday to the study of history, another hour to reading works on teaching or education, and half an hour each morning and evening to the preparation for his daily recitations, and the remainder of his leisure time to general reading, recreation and exercise. The time usually spent in loafing at the village store, or in idle conversation, would be better consumed in general reading, such as newspapers, magazines, even fiction. I would advise the teacher to be careful what fictitious works he reads. The standard authors as Dickens, Scott, Mrs. Stowe, may be dipped into lightly, but too much time spent even in reading the best and purest works of fiction is but wasted. Remember that you have a life-time in which to read these works, and do not be in a hurry to finish them. Use them as a means of mental relaxation, but do not be carried away by them. If you find they are absorbing too much of your attention, stop and lay them aside. Better even never read fiction at all if you find you can not control your appetite for it. You are driving a fast team, and you need keep a tight rein. There is plenty of interesting general reading to occupy your leisure besides fiction. Read works of travel, biographies, historical works, and miscellaneous sketches and you will find yourself better informed, and at the same time rested from more active labors. If you can take up a work of fiction, and read a few minutes, and then lay it down without an effort, you are perfectly safe, but if it absorbs so much of your mind, and excites your imagination so much that you will sit up half a night to finish a novel, you would better never look inside of one. I was once a whole year reading one of Dickens' novels, and I am positive that it did me more good than if I had read it in two days or two weeks. I have done a great deal of light reading while walking to and from school, but as this is hard on the eyes, I would not recommend it. Perhaps if not more than five or ten minutes at a time is spent in this way, no harm can result to the eyes. It is a good plan to carry a book with you, and read a page or two, and then with your eyes off the book, resting them, think over what you have read. Consider for a moment what may be accomplished in this way. You may read a page in a minute, and ten pages each day will amount to a large book at the end of the year. If you are enthusiastic you will always carry a book or magazine with you, and read while waiting for your meals, for the train, anywhere and everywhere opportunity presents to occupy a few moments in this way. This may sound trifling, but remember that, "trifles light as air make up the sum of human things," and "little drops of water, little grains of sand, make the mighty ocean, and the bounteous land."

The teacher needs a general knowledge not only to enable him to teach well, but enable him to fill a high place in society. But almost every man has some special talent in some direction, a special love and talent for some science or art and this he should cultivate. Do you take more interest in Geology than any other science, then commence a collection of specimens and use every opportunity to inform yourself in this specialty. If it is Botany, collect a herbarium. If Chemistry, get a few chemicals and apparatus and go to experimenting. If you have a talent for Music or Painting, cultivate it.

In general, let the teacher make ample preparation for his work, and though he do not follow it for a lifetime, the culture he receives will be of inestimable value in whatever profession or walk of life he may choose or be driven to accept. Do not think that because you are only a country teacher that you need no special training or that you will never amount to anything in the world. Some of the greatest statesmen and scientists, poets and authors of this country began their career as teachers of country schools.

V. THE SPIRIT OF THE TEACHER.

Every person who enters the sacred temple of the school-room for the purpose of assuming control of the young and budding minds which daily assemble for instruction, should make a careful self-examination and inquire what are his motives and what the spirit which prompts him to such a step. Is it for money alone? Is it for popularity? Is it because he is unfitted for any other occupation? Is it because he loves to display his knowledge? If he has no higher motives than these he would better for the sake of those who are to be under his care and for his own sake, enlist in the army, go to the poor-house or run off to sea.

I can not better express what I wish my readers to know than in the language of an old and prominent educator whose " *Theory and Practice of Teaching* " was of great value to me in my first years of teaching. I refer to David P. Page, who says, " But the *true spirit of the teacher*,—a spirit that seeks not alone pecuniary emolument, but desires to be in the highest degree useful to those who are taught; a spirit that elevates above everything else the nature and capabilities of the human soul, and that trembles under the responsibility of attempting to be its educator; a spirit that looks upon gold as the contemptible dross of the earth, when compared with that imperishable gem which is to be polished and brought out into heaven's light to shine forever; a spirit that scorns all the rewards of earth and seeks that highest of all rewards, an approving conscience and an approving God; a spirit that earnestly inquires what is right, and that dreads to do what is wrong; a spirit that can recognize and reverence the handiwork of God in every child, and that burns with the desire to be instrumental in training it to the highest attainment of which it is capable,—*such a spirit* is the first thing to be sought by the teacher, and without it the highest talent can not make him truly excellent in his profession."

Cultivate such a spirit and with a good moral character, with good mental and physical endowments you will be in the highest degree successful. There are many who make teaching the stepping-stone to some more lucrative employment or profession. I can not say that this is altogether wrong. While it is true that experience makes good teachers, and men who have been a life-time trying to improve themselves in the art of teaching are generally the best teachers, yet experience is not really necessary to make a good teacher. If a young man throws his whole soul into the work and has the proper qualifications he may teach as well the first school he undertakes as he would after forty years' experience. He may profit by the experience and mistakes of others. The trouble is not so much that men make teaching a stepping-stone to something else, but it lies in the fact that men do not learn to do with their might what they find to do. A young man may be preparing for the law, medicine or the ministry, and at the same time be wholly and heartily enlisted in the work of teaching. If we consider the matter aright a man should be a teacher in any profession and he who does his best while teaching will be very apt to do his best in whatever other profession he may afterwards choose. In other words, if he have the true spirit of the teacher he will have the true spirit of the lawyer, physician or minister.

VI. PERSONAL HABITS.

If men were perfectly well balanced morally, mentally and physically, perhaps they would have no bad habits; but be that as it may, a few words here in regard to the habits of the teacher will not be out of place. The power of habit is great, but there are few men who have habits which they can not break, and every man can cultivate good habits. Do you use tobacco? Break it off when you enter the profession of teacher. You can do it. All you have to do is to quit. If you have not the moral stamina to say to yourself, I will not be ruled by habit, you are not fit for a teacher. Of course, no one who pretends in this day to teach, uses ardent spirits, at least they are so few that I need not say anything about it here.

As the following points have been touched upon elsewhere, I wish merely to call attention under this head to some of the good habits the teacher should endeavor to cultivate.

1. *Neatness of person and dress.* The teacher should dress well, not necessarily in costly garments but neatly, plainly, and according to his circumstances. A threadbare coat even if "out at the elbows" will look well with a clean, well-laundried shirt and collar, a neat neck tie and clean, polished boots or shoes. All flashy, foppish costume is out of place upon the teacher. The morning ablution of face and hands, neck and ears and attention to the finger nails and teeth are of importance to neatness of appearance. Cutting and cleaning the

finger nails and picking the teeth are improper in company. A frequent use of a clothes brush to remove dust and spots of grease, and of a hair brush to remove dandruff is necessary. *No person can be clean and use tobacco.*

He who is neat of person and dress will necessarily try to keep the school-room neat and clean.

2. *System and regularity.* Let everything the teacher does be done in a regular and systematic manner. This habit once fixed is of incalculable importance. Nearly all men who have made a name and fortune in business will tell you that they owed much of their success to the habit of doing everything according to system. (See p. 12).

3. *Politeness.* This is one of the necessary habits of the teacher. The true teacher is ever the true gentleman. He will be polite and courteous in manner and in language. True politeness has its origin in love. He who loves his fellow man as the Saviour commanded will ever be polite. It is the spontaneous overflow of a generous and noble spirit. The teacher who posesses this quality will exercise politeness to all with whom he comes in contact. He will have a word for everybody, and a kind look and engaging manner towards children. His conversation will not be polluted with slang, nor poisoned with profanity.

4. *Punctuality.* This habit should be studiously cultivated. If the teacher is not prompt and punctual he can not expect his pupils to be. He should carry this habit into everything he undertakes. Be punctual to all engagments, whether to meet a friend, to attend church,

to business matters, to school duties, or in whatever you may have to do with your fellow man.

5. *Studiousness.* Study must be made a habit. Assign certain stated times for study, and conscientiously devote the required time to it. You must study every day, if it is only a little.

VII. IN RELATION TO PATRONS.

The highest duty of man is to please God, next to please his fellow man and lastly to please himself. The majority of men, perhaps, reverse this order in practice. But if a man do right he will please God, all good men and himself. A great responsibility rests upon the teacher. He is placed in charge of a number of human beings, young, inexperienced, of impressible and elastic nature, capable of being moulded, bended at the will of the operator. He holds these beings in trust and is responsible for their well-being and advancement while under his care. It is true a teacher has a hard task and too much is often expected of him. When children are without moral or mental training at home and inherit passions and appetites from vicious parents, it is not to be supposed the teacher during the comparatively short time they are under his care, should reform and change their nature. But much can be done towards this result and the most earnest worker will accomplish the most.

The teacher should endeavor to please his patrons. In order to do this his patrons should be acquainted with his plans and modes of work. Every parent in the district should be visited at least once during the term of school and if possible every parent should be induced to visit the school. The teacher should anticipate any trouble which may arise between him and the parents, visit them and talk the matter over, and if possible, nip the trouble in the bud. If the child brings any orders or instructions to the teacher from the parent, the teacher should at once visit that parent and talk the matter over and come to a fair understanding. In nine cases out of ten, the parent will yield to the teacher's plans and approve of them, where otherwise if the teacher had gone on, and done as he thought best without consulting the parent, he would have made an enemy of him, much to his subsequent regret. There should be a perfect understanding between teacher and patron, and perfect cooperation in the plans of teacher and school board.

The country teacher will find all kinds of men to deal with. He will find mercenary, close-fisted school directors, who will grudge him his wages, and will not listen to any demands for expenditures in regard to the school or school-house. He will find directors who are careless and indifferent to the matter, who will not express an opinion in regard to his plans, tell him to go ahead and do as he thinks best, but if any trouble arises, in which their children are concerned, they will be the first to make complaint and spread evil reports about the teacher. He will find men who are continually meddling and causing trouble in the school. He will find families who, having feuds among themselves, will carry them into the school-room, and the teacher will be put to his wit's end to manage matters. He will find the north end of the district arrayed against the south end, a village part against the country part of a district, political troubles, differences among rich and poor, all of which will affect the welfare of his school. The teacher then needs to be a tactician of high order. He should be ever on the watch-tower to foresee these difficulties and devise some means to meet them.

The teacher should make himself familiar with his patrons, take an interest in their business, not in a meddling manner, but that he may converse with them on topics with which they are familiar. Let him talk to the farmer about his crops, to the stock raiser or dealer about his cattle and hogs, to the mechanic about his work, &c. Let him not be too ready to communicate knowledge, but rather be a good listener, and by a few judicious questions lead them to do the greater part of the talking. In this way he will make himself agreeable to his patrons, and they can not have reason to think he feels above them. Poor people and many country people are very sensitive on this point and are often ready to think a man feels himself above them when no such thing is true. In many localities there is nothing that people so much detest as what they style a "big-feeling" person or a "big-head." A teacher in the country must have a good deal of the "do-as-the-Romans-do" feeling in order to succeed. St. Paul said, "I was all things to all men, that I might win some." So it must be with the teacher to a certain extent. (See p. 13).

A few words in this connection about making application for a school will not be inappropriate. The teacher has here an opportunity to try his tact. I do not mean that he should try his skill in driving a sharp bargain although it is sometimes necessary, for school boards will hire a teacher as they would buy a pair of shoes, but I mean that he should so adapt himself to circumstances that he may make the most favorable impression upon the men with whom he is dealing.

To illustrate I will at the risk of seeming egotistic, relate a bit of my own experience in this line. I had just been attending a Normal school in the vicinity and the school boards in that section had been imposed upon in a number of instances by young men who attending this school and having run short of funds, attempted to raise them by seeking employment in the neighborhood as teachers. Of course I was asked immediately if I had been a student of said school and on answering in the affirmative was met with the rebuff that I was not wanted. Before coming to the next man I determined to change my tactics. It was harvest time and I found the men busy in the field. I climbed over the fence and began binding wheat until I came up to the men. Having found the director, I kept on at work while talking to him. He never thought of inquiring whether I was from that school but I was told afterwards that I had created a favorable impression because I seemed not to be afraid of work. I contracted for that school at my own figures. I do not give this as a model way of applying for a school but to illustrate the power of tact. Remember that tact outweighs talent very often. Show that you mean business and do not display any disposition to yield to the desire for a cheap teacher. Teachers themselves are very often to blame for their low wages. If they would use a little of the shrewdness used by the farmer selling a horse the standard of wages would increase. In the first place you should qualify yourself to teach and then rate your services sufficiently high. A poor teacher is like poor butter, dear at any price.

Always make a written contract. In some places it

is required by boards of education; in others merely a verbal contract is all that is asked.

VIII. IN RELATION TO SOCIETY.

The teacher should be a model man in the community in which he moves. If he has all the requirements of a true teacher, he will be a model man, and very little more need be said on this point. He should be eminently of a social disposition, and mingle much with society. It is proper to see the teacher take a part in social parties, in the Sunday school, in church, in all meetings and organizations which are for the public good. He should not, however, show a partisan or sectarian spirit, nor on the other hand, attempt to please all by carrying water on both shoulders. But let him be straightforward, candid and honest in his views and utterances. He may have his political creed and religious creed but it is not well to make much of a display of either. Let him show the teacher in all that he does, teaching both by example and precept, not intruding his services but ready and willing at all times to respond to the public desire. He should be above those little envies and jealousies which abound in some communities. He should have none of that disposition which finds utterance in the expression, "If I can not have the best place I do not want any." He should have none of the "rule or ruin" policy. (See p. 13).

IX. IN RELATION TO THE PROFESSION.

"Iron sharpeneth iron." The teacher should come frequently in contact with others of his class. He can learn something from every teacher. Let him visit other schools and observe the work of other teachers. He will not fail to find something to model after or see something to avoid. His own faults may be repeated by some one else and by seeing them in others he is more apt to see that they *are* faults. He may learn much by conversing with other teachers, especially with those who have had more experience, and he should seek opportunity to converse with such teachers.

He should attend and take part in teachers' institutes and associations. The country teachers are too apt to stand back and the city teachers who generally conduct such institutes willingly permit them to do so. We hear the frequent complaint that institutes are of little benefit to country teachers. It is only too true. The plans and methods there discussed and presented by prominent educators are rarely applicable to the country school. Many of the institute lecturers are men who never taught in a country school, or if they did it was many years before, and the ideas they have are such as they have acquired by reading or theorizing in their study-rooms. These men will take a class of young men and women and proceed to instruct them as though they were small children, expecting to exhibit in this way their modes of instructing children. Did it never occur to any of them or to their hearers that if a class of real children were before them matters might not proceed so smoothly? Some of these prominent institute instructors I fear would not make a success of a school in a back-woods district.

A good plan for country teachers would be to organize township institutes and instruct each other. Let them be something of the nature of a medical society, consisting of free interchange of thought and opinion in the form of essays, orations, debates, &c. If all the teachers of a township can not be brought together, let any half dozen or more teachers organize themselves into a society and meet once or twice a month on Saturdays at convenient places. Much good might be done in this way. I am appealing now to the reader of this book to work up something of this kind in his neighborhood. You can do it and you ought to do it. Large sums are annually expended in almost every county for prominent instructors at teachers' institues. Does the outlay pay? It undoubtedly pays the instructors but I fear the country teacher is paying a big price to hear a "big gun" which makes but little more than noise after all. These local or township societies will cost scarcely anything and will be of undoubted value to the teachers.

CHAPTER II.

THE SCHOOL.

I. PRELIMINARY WORK.

THE teacher's work begins the moment he has contracted for the school. He should endeavor first to learn something of the nature of the school he is about to undertake. This knowledge he may obtain from the parents, from the former teachers, and possibly, from the children themselves. Spend a week or more in getting acquainted with the parents and pupils. You need not use any formality but drop into their homes and chat with them. You will learn all sorts of things about the school in an indirect manner and without asking many questions. They will be ready to tell you all about the school as conducted the previous term and about the bad pupils and what parents are meddlesome and you will hear all sorts of opinions about the former teacher. You can then make up some opinion from this evidence, conflicting though it may be. You should visit the school-house and find out what repairs or apparatus may be needed and kindly ask the Directors to have things in order before school commences. You should unfold to them your plans and, if possible, obtain their promise of co-operation. If possible, see or correspond with the previous teacher and learn from him his plans and such knowledge of the school as he may be able to give.

There is nothing like making a good beginning. Having found out what kind of a school you are likely to have and what branches will be studied, you can have a programme made out before entering the school. Of course it may be necessary to make changes in the programme, but it is best to have one made out in general form before the first day of school.

A programme will vary according to the number and character of the branches taught and somewhat according to the number of pupils in the school. The teacher is required by law to teach so many hours. I would advise a teacher to be prompt and punctual to time, not teaching any more nor any less than the required time. Schools in the country usually begin at 9 o'clock and close at 4 with one hour for noon and two recesses of 15 minutes each. I have here a programme which provides within the time allotted, space for all the branches usually taught in the country school. It is a programme both of recitation and study, and for convenience I have divided the school into three grades on the subject of reading. The A grade consists of the 1st, 2nd, and 3rd Readers; the B grade of the 4th and 5th Readers, and the C grade of the 6th Reader. The words in **bold faced type** denote recitations; in common type, studies. It is supposed that part of the advanced lessons will be prepared outside of school hours. It will be objected, perhaps, by some that the time allotted to recitations is too short. I answer that I have been obliged to teach all the above branches within the allotted time and of course had to do the best I could. If there are not so many branches, then more time can be allowed to the others. I have here provided for the extreme cases. It will be observed that there is no time for a Primary Grammar class. The reader is referred to the chapter on Grammar for an explanation. I have grouped all beginners in reading as the Primer class. During the winter months in some schools there will be none to represent this class, none but can read in the 1st Reader. The programme is so arranged that the very small pupils may be dismissed half an hour earlier than the others; also, that they can be allowed to go out and play in fine weather after they have recited. It will be seen that the time to study a lesson is provided, so far as possible, immediately after the recitation. This should be insisted on from the beginning.

The grades A, B and C are only here given for convenience in arranging the programme. They are not absolute divisions of the school. As a general rule those placed in the B grade will study Primary Geography, Arithmetic to about as far as Fractions and be in the Primary Spelling class; but some who are in this grade may study Grammar, Advanced Geography, History, or Physiology, and some who are in the C grade may be in a Primary Geography class or Primary Spelling class. These grades are, therefore, only arbitrary divisions necessary to form a programme both of study and recitation. Many pupils may belong to two of the grades.

IN COUNTRY SCHOOLS. 37

PROGRAMME OF RECITATION AND STUDY:

TIME.			A GRADE.	B GRADE.	C GRADE.
Begins	Ends	Continues.			
5:	9:5	5	GENERAL EXERCISES.		
9:5	9:15	10	Primer Class		
9:15	9:25	10	1st Reader	Spelling	Spelling
9:25	9:35	10	2nd Reader		History
9:35	9:45	10	3rd Reader		
9:45	9:50	5		Rest.	
9:50	10:5	15	Slates & Blocks	4th Reader	Advanced Geo;.
10:5	10:20	15	Reading	Prim. Geog.	
10:20	10:35	15		Recess.	
10:35	10:45	10	Primer Class		
10:45	11	15	Slates & Blocks	Primary Geog.	Grammar
11	11:15	15			Algebra
11:15	11:20	5		Rest.	
11:20	11:35	15	Reading	5th Reader	Grammar
11:35	15	25		Arithmetic	
12	1	60		NOON.	
1	1:10	10	Primer Class		
1:10	1:20	10	1st Reader		
1:20	1:30	10	2nd Reader	Reading	Arithmetic
1:30	1:40	10	3rd Reader		
1:40	1:55	15	Slates & Blocks		6th Reader
1:55	2	5		Rest.	
2	2:15	15	Blackboard	Arithmetic	Adv Geog.
2:15	2:30	15	Reading		Physiology
2:30	2:45	15		Recess.	
2:45	3	15		Prim Spell'g.	
3	3:15	15	Slates & Blocks	Arithmetic	Adv. Spelling
3:15	3:30	15			U. S. History
3:30	3:45	15	Dismissed	Writing	Writing
3:45	4	15		Reading	Arithmetic

II. ORGANIZING.

If the preliminary work detailed in the previous section be attended to, the work of organizing will be materially lessened. You should spend but little time organizing and getting ready for active work. You should commence at once with an explanation of the programme. That all may have something to do you should assign a lesson for each class, something not very difficult but which will occupy their attention a short time at least. The time allotted on programme for general exercises will be sufficient for explanation of programme and assigning lessons and then you are ready to begin the recitations. Have a little book in which to enroll the names of the pupils of each class when they have taken their places at the recitation seats. By enrolling their names in this way by classes you will the sooner become acquainted with the individual pupils, and it is not so embarrassing as taking a general enrollment of the whole school at once. Go strictly according to programme. Do not vary a minute. Commence this the first day and continue it until the last. Not very much in the way of study need be expected the first day and consequently the recitation time can be taken up in preliminary drills on the next lesson, in enrolling names and in familiar talk about their studies. The time on programme denoted "Rest" you can occupy the first day in general remarks on your plan of government, the necessity of system and order in the school, &c.

See that every pupil has a slate and pencil. If all have not, ask them if they will not try and get the mas soon as possible. Attend, also, to the matter of getting books.

If you commence in this way as though you meant business and thoroughly understood your business, you will create a good impression among your pupils the first day and this is a point of great value. As it becomes necessary you may make slight changes in the programme but frequent changes should be avoided and they may be, if you have well studied the matter before hand. I have often heard teachers remark that they always dreaded the first and last days of school. In regard to the first day if they would prepare themselves as I have suggested before coming to the school-house and then commence actual business at once, the first day need not be a source of dread.

Any lengthy speeches or remarks about the former school, or boasting of what you expect to accomplish are out of place not only the first day, but every other day of the school.

III. CONDUCTING RECITATIONS.

As much will be said on this subject in connection with the methods of teaching the various branches, a few general observations will be all that is necessary here.

The success of a teacher depends in the largest measure upon the manner in which he conducts a recitation. Remember that it is one thing to *hear* a class recite and another to conduct a recitation properly. Under the ancient regime we heard of a *Master* who *kept* school and *heard* his scholars recite. Now it is, or should be, a *Teacher* who *teaches* his pupils.

The objects of a recitation may be grouped under four heads as follows:

1. Examination.
2. Instruction.
3. Cultivation.
4. Excitation.

1. It is to be supposed the pupil has studied his lesson and the first object is to find out what he knows about it. This information is necessary for several reasons. The teacher must know what the pupil has learned in order to assign further lessons and give additional instruction. The pupil by rehearsing what he has learned fixes it in his memory and cultivates the

power of expression and receives instruction from his fellow pupils. The first thing is the examination of the written work previously prepared by the pupils. This may be accompanied with instruction, encouragement, criticism or censure. Next the teacher should test the knowledge of the pupils by calling for reports on topics, by questions judiciously put, by written work on blackboard or slates, by reviews, drills, &c. Questions are advantageously used and also abused by teachers. As a general thing leading questions or such as suggest the answer, should be avoided. If used, they should be only for young pupils or for reviews or as an occasional concert drill. Questions should be so put as to lead the pupil to think and answer them in his own language. Pupils should not be called upon in rotation, but promiscuously. This secures better attention and bars the possibility of special preparation for special parts of the lesson to the neglect of other parts. When called upon to report on a topic it is generally best that a pupil rise to his feet, especially if the class is large.

The importance of constant reviewing can not be overestimated. A review of the lesson of the previous day should be had each day. This need not occupy much time as only the leading points of the lesson should be reviewed. Not only should each lesson be reviewed, but not less than once a week there should be a general review of all passed over since the last review, and once a month or so there should be a general review of the whole subject from the beginning. Review lessons may be given occasionally, requiring written answers to questions placed on the black-board by the teacher.

2. It is the office of the teacher to impart additional information. Much of this may be done in preliminary drills. The teacher should be a treasure house of information on each branch he teaches. He can be this by constant study of the lessons previous to the recitations and by being a general reader and making notes of what he reads. Every teacher should have a blank book in which to note down anything and everything which may have a possible bearing on the branches he expects to teach. There are many points of interest which may be learned from newspapers, magazines and journals, encyclopedias, works of biography, history and travel, and in larger treatises on the same subjects of the class books, which should be noted down under the proper heads convenient for reference. Among these points are such as follows: In Arithmetic, short methods of solving examples, curious properties of numbers, history and origin of figures, test examples. In Geography, popular names of states, cities and countries, origin and meaning of names, historical incidents connected with places or countries, remarkable natural curiosities, manners and customs of the people, recent political changes, and much other matter not found in the text-books. In Grammar, disposition of difficult constructions, outlines, remarks on the history and origin of language, &c. In History, incidents not found in text-books popular names and appellations of men, biographical sketches, points in the philosophy of history, recent events, &c. In Natural Science, any easy experiment, or remarkable or interesting fact. In general, the teacher should note down any thought which may come to him at odd times, or any observation dropped from the lips of others on the methods of teaching, governing, or managing a school, or any information obtained from lectures, political speeches or sermons which would have a bearing on his school work. Such a book will prove in a few years a mine of gold to any teacher. Also let him make a scrap-book, and from every newspaper he can get hold of cull fragments of value, and paste them in it. It is remarkable what may be done in a few years in this way. I have a scrap-book which no money would buy and it has not cost me one cent of outlay. I have fragments which I have been gathering for ten years and now it is a volume of history, biography, poetry, literature, science and art. It is my plan to cut out of every paper which I can get hold of, whether it is one I subscribe for or a stray copy given me, or one which has been wrapped around goods, or one picked up in the street; I cut out I say everything useful or interesting and then sort them over and put in scrap-book those of most value, classifying them under the proper heads.

But the teacher must not be a lecturer. He may talk too much. It is not the amount of information given, but the amount imbibed which counts. Give a little at each recitation and let no recitation pass without a little, but avoid prolixity.

He should be ready in the use of familiar illustrations and should cultivate the power of explanation. To do this he must study his lesson before coming to the class. Prof. Alfred Holbrook used to say there were three grades of teaching power; 1st and lowest, the power to make the brightest pupils understand; 2nd, the power to make the majority of the class understand, and 3rd, and highest power was to make the dullest pupil in the class understand. Study, teacher, to attain to this highest grade of teaching power.

The teacher will also instruct the pupil how to study a lesson and carefully direct his studies. This should be done at the close of a recitation as a preliminary drill for the next lesson.

3. The teacher should seek by the recitation to cultivate accurate and fluent expression in writing and speaking. The pupils have prepared written work at their seats. By careful examination and just criticism the teacher can aid the pupil to cultivate his power of expressing himself in writing. Spelling, Capitals, Punctuation, Syntax, Arrangement, Method, Neatness, &c., should be carefully noted. In speaking, also, the pupil should be cultivated in throwing off embarrassment, and in the use of good language.

He should seek to cultivate in his pupils habits of attention. Much may be done in this respect by mutual criticisms. Care should be taken, however, that it is not overdone. Ill feeling is sometimes the result of pupils criticising each other, and among small pupils much confusion in the class results unless it is carefully controlled by the teacher. A good plan to cultivate attention is to call frequently for a report or repetition of some explanation or information given by teacher or any of the pupils. For example, the teacher imparts to-day some information not given in the text-book, and to-morrow calls for a repetition of it from the class. This is an excellent exercise.

4. Under the head of Excitation, (I beg pardon for using an unfamiliar word, but I could find no other which

would so well express my meaning), I wish to speak of the teacher's duty to arouse an interest in study, excite a love for study and lead the pupil into channels of independent thought and investigation.

He must arouse an interest and excite a love for study by a careful attention to the previous points in this section. In addition, the teacher should be full of enthusiasm. The pupils will imbibe this feeling in a measure from the teacher. They will not likely be interested in their work unless the teacher is interested in his work. This holy enthusiasm is one of the main points of distinguishing a true and good teacher from a dull and lifeless and inferior teacher.

He should lead his pupils into new pastures of independent thought and original investigation by judicious questions and directions, and by assigning appropriate topics. Timid and slow pupils should be encouraged by kind words and favorable comments.

IV. GOVERNMENT.

Volumes have been written on this topic alone. I propose to make a very short treatise answer my purpose. If a teacher teach well he will have but little governing to do. The tap root of a system of government in school is to furnish all with employment that is interesting to them and at the same time conducive to their highest mental and moral development. To keep the imps of mischief away, put the angel of business on guard. This is the Pestalozzian idea. Hear what this great pioneer of education had to say on this subject: "If from the imperfection of his reasoning powers, or his want of knowledge of facts, the child is not able to enter into the sense or follow the chain of ideas; if he is made to repeat what to him is sound without sense, it is not strange that he becomes restless and disobedient." The great mistake of too many teachers is that they expect too much of children. They proceed too much on the presumption that a child has the mind of a man and will be interested in abstract subjects. You must not only furnish him something to do, but it must be something he can do and will like to do. Then he will have business and will have no time nor inclination for mischief. Nothing is naturally more active than the human mind, and especially the mind of a child. It craves and seeks after knowledge. If not properly directed it seeks after the bad as well as after the good, and we are most of us inclined to think that it is more apt to seek after the bad. Place a child in a church during a sermon and watch his actions, and by recalling our own experience when a child we can easily imagine his thoughts. He is not interested in the sermon because he can not understand it. He soon grows tired seeing the people and he shifts his position a hundred times, counts the panes of glass in the windows, looks at the ceiling and out the window and tries every possible way to interest himself except to get into downright mischief, which he longs to do, and would do, were it not for parental restraint or the awe of the place and the restraint of the people around him. A child goes to school and is placed on a seat with others of like dispositions and like restless minds. There is not the awe of a church nor dread of parents' frown nor dignity of numerous older heads to restrain him. He is assigned a lesson which in great part may as well be for all he can understand of it, a portion of Homer's Illiad in the original Greek. Can you expect anything else than mischief from the child, especially if he has an active mind? There are some children so dull and stupid that they never give the teacher any trouble, and when grown up will never agitate the world. It is from the child which, if not furnished with employment, would fall into mischief that the world must expect its "coming man."

Remember then, teacher, that here is where you must begin to lay your foundation of government. This is the solid rock on which you must build. If you succeed perfectly in this you will have but little else to do. With a large school you can not succeed perfectly in keeping all employed, but you should do all you can toward this end.

The teacher should teach pupils to govern themselves, and only when his best endeavors to this end fail should he resort to coercive measures. Were children properly trained from infancy up there would never be any need of force in governing them. But the teacher has not had the charge of these children from infancy, and in nine cases out of ten if he had had them in charge he would have failed to train them properly. Consequently, considering the frailties of human nature, force sometimes becomes a necessity in the managing of youth.

A Republican or Democratic form of government is undoubtedly the best for Nations or communities, and, to a certain extent, it is best in the school-room; but there must be a slight savoring of despotism. The teacher should be, to some extent, the autocrat of the school-room. He should endeavor to lay before the school a few fundamental principles of government, and as far as possible, secure the voice of the majority in enacting and enforcing requirements. But there may be cases where it is necessary for the teacher to use his own mind without appealing to the pupils for sanction. He should explain to them at the first that as all came there to be instructed, it is to the highest interest of all that the teacher's whole time should be spent in teaching, and that if every one would attend only to the work necessary to acquire knowledge, there would be no necessity for government.

The teacher, while he does not make a show of watching his pupils, should ever be on the alert to detect departures from propriety and at once check them. A firm stand at the beginning is of great importance. One evil act if permitted to pass unnoticed will be followed by a score. A rather rigid discipline at first will prevent the necessity of close watching afterward.

The teacher need say but little about government. A system of rules laid down is of more harm than good. The general principle, *Do Right* is all the rule necessary. Let the teacher be orderly and systematic in everything he undertakes and he will thus unconsciously teach order and system to his pupils.

Do not attempt to keep a school as still as a church is when the minister is praying. The performance of the actual duties of the school-room, if carried on in an enthusiastic manner, can not be without more or less noise. But you should endeavor to check unnecessary noise. Do not expect too much of the pupils. Consider that forty pupils will make more noise than twenty, and if any one points you to a quiet school, ask how many pupils there are. I have seen teachers who kept forty and fifty pupils almost as still as death, but I never saw very much real progress made in studies under such teachers. They were a success so far as keeping a school quiet was concerned, and that was all. Shall whispering be suppressed? Yes, and no. If it is injuring the school, suppress as far as you can. Some claim they can suppress it entirely, but I do not believe it. It is one of the impossibilities, especially if you do any teaching at the same time. If a school is small and pupils study and recite well, I can not see what harm there can be in whispering a little. If a pupil has plenty of work to do he will not spend much time in whispering. If a school is large and the pupils crowded, a great deal of confusion will result if each pupil only whispers a little. In such cases the teacher will explain the necessity of refraining from whispering and do all in his power to check it. He may find it necessary to deprive those who persist in this practice of a part of their recesses. With many merely calling their attention to the fact will be all that is necessary. With some it will have a good effect to write their names on the black-board. All this should be done not so much as a punishment, but as a reminder of the fact that they are disturbing the school, and the teacher should so explain. Extreme cases may require extreme remedies, and I leave the teacher to devise his own mode of punishment.

As was said in the beginning of this section, if all are employed very little in the way of government will be necessary. It behooves the teacher, therefore, to devise ways and means to keep all from the largest to the smallest employed profitably and pleasurably. He who succeeds best in this will succeed best in governing his school. Let me make a few suggestions in this matter. With large pupils the question of employment will not be a difficult one. Provide plenty of written work in each of the branches they pursue and by properly conducted recitations and judicious assignment of lessons, all the older pupils will be kept properly employed. If any wide-awake, active boys or girls are well up with their lessons it will not be improper to allow them to read some book or paper in school hours. Many a mischievously inclined boy may be diverted from the mischief he would fall into, by simply requesting him to bring an armful of wood, a bucket of coal, or a pail of water. Some pupils are naturally so full of life, that unless they are employed constantly, they will naturally fall into mischief. Such children are sometimes the brightest in the school. Their surplus energies need only to be directed in the right channel. Like the locomotive, they are a power for good so long as kept on the track, but let them get off the track, and they are a power for mischief. Such pupils may be requested to write their spelling or reading lessons, or place the solution of an example on the blackboard. I do not like to see a child who has not enough energy about him to get into mischief. The teacher will be ever on the watch for something useful to act as a safety valve for such vivacious pupils. There is a point worth thinking of right here, teachers, a lead, which if followed, will yield rich results in the way of managing such pupils. (See pp. 45 and 46).

No pupil, old or young, should come to school without a slate. The teacher should attend to this matter, and if he cannot induce parents to purchase slates, it will pay him in the way of securing order in the school-room, to buy them, and loan them to the pupils. A little talk with the parents in regard to the matter, will, however, usually secure them. There is no one thing that will aid so much in keeping pupils occupied as slates. The reading and spelling classes will find them a necessity in writing or printing their spelling lists, and very young pupils, in drawing, printing letters, and making figures. The teacher should keep the young pupils busy with slates and blocks. Simple drawing lessons should be placed on the blackboard, such as any teacher can draw, whether he has ever studied drawing or not, as squares, triangles, rectangles, parallel lines, stars, boxes, the simple outline of a house, a barrel, a cup, &c. Blocks are another means of government. Let the teacher go to some mechanic's shop, and if he has ordinary ingenuity, he can, out of a few pieces of pine board, make a set of blocks which can be used by both small and large pupils; by small pupils to play with, and by large ones to represent square and cube root, mensuration of solids, &c. Let him make a cube, to illustrate cube root, a pyramid, a triangular prism, a parallelopiped, a cylinder, a cone, &c. Also, a number of blocks in the shape and proportion of bricks, but they need not be more than three inches in length. If the teacher cannot make these himself, it will cost but a trifle to get a mechanic to make them. Very young pupils can be kept employed for hours in building houses, &c., with these blocks. To prevent making noise, by the falling of the blocks on the desk, I have sometimes spread a shawl or a couple of newspapers over the desk. Blocks with the alphabet can be purchased for a small sum, and will be very convenient and useful.

During warm weather the very young pupils should be allowed to play out of doors after they have recited their lessons and practiced for a few minutes with slates, but in winter this can not be, and some means must be used to keep them employed. They may be allowed to draw and print on the black-board as an occasional exercise for a change. Children are generally fond of marking with chalk. Every school-house should be provided with plenty of black-board. (See p. 60).

Pupils get tired sitting still and thus grow restless. For this reason I have provided in the programme intervals of five minutes which I have denominated "*Rest.*" Rest is not necessarily absolute cessation from activity. Rest is only change. These intervals may be used in various ways. To check whispering I have given these five-minute intervals for that purpose, allowing the pupils to move about the room but not permitting them to leave it nor to indulge in boisterous play, but that they may stretch their limbs and have a few minutes for conversation. These intervals may be used in giving calisthenic exercises, if thought proper, or the teacher may give oral drills to the whole school on some subject of natural science, or read or relate a story, or sometimes it is necessary to talk to the whole school on some matter pertaining to government, or about something that has occurred in school. I would not have any set programme for these intervals, but occupy them sometimes in one way and sometimes in another. Variety is the spice of life and we cannot get along without it. If a visitor enters your school do not interrupt the usual course of your work but adhere strictly to the programme, and when the time for "Rest" comes then you may ask him to talk to your school or spend the five minutes in talking to him.

The five minutes in the morning denominated "General Exercise," may be also used in various ways. Exercises may be given which will go far towards securing punctual attendance. Read a portion of some interesting story each morning, always leaving off in an interesting place, or give short lectures on some scientific subject, or the time may be devoted to matters of business as announcing special lessons, arranging pupils seats or providing for a new pupil.

A strict attention to these seemingly small matters will go far towards securing good order in school.

Very small pupils should not spend the whole day in school, but as this is a matter to be settled between the teacher and parents, I can only ask the teacher to try and make such arrangements with parents so that the small pupils can be dismissed an hour or two before the rest. Some parents will even object to allowing small pupils to play out of doors during school hours, but if this matter is explained by the teacher no trouble will ensue, and if they are consulted in reference to sending small pupils home the matter can generally be arranged. The only objection to this is in the fact that some children have a long way to go to school, and very small children need the company and protection of their older brothers and sisters.

There is no sense nor propriety in keeping small children a whole day in school. It is imposing too much upon the teacher of an ungraded school. He is obliged to teach everything from the Alphabet to Algebra and manage all ages from five years old to twenty, and I do not see the need of keeping the little ones confined several hours longer than is necessary for their instruction. Therefore, every teacher should try to make such arrangements with school boards and parents as will remedy this matter.

To recapitulate the matter of government:

1. Let the teacher teach well.

2. Let him set an example of order and system by being orderly and systematic himself.

3. Let him provide means to keep all profitably and pleasantly employed.

4. Let him secure the aid of parents and school boards and work in harmony with them.

5. Let him be calm, watchful and firm.

I can not forbear closing this chapter with an extract from Herbert Spencer: "The independent English boy is father of the independent English man; and you cannot have the last without the first. German teachers say that they had rather manage a dozen German boys than one English one. Shall we, therefore, wish that our boys had the manageableness of the German ones, and with it the submissiveness and political serfdom of adult Germans? Or, shall we not rather tolerate in our boys those feelings which make them free men, and modify our methods accordingly?" What Spencer says of the English boy can only be more emphatically said of the American boy. That independent spirit which will not take off the hat to a Prince sooner than to a beggar, requires a different kind of government from that necessary for that cringing, servile submissiveness which characterizes too many of the Old World inhabitants.

As self-government prevails in our Nation, so it should prevail in the family and school. If properly taught here it will be easy there, and we need not fear a downfall of our Republic so long as the principles on which it is based are taught in the family and school. If it is high-minded men who constitute a state, it is the teacher's duty to make high-minded men out of the boys under his control, and thus be the greatest benefactor of the race. Ruskin told his country-men to set their minds upon multiplying Englishmen. Let us set our minds upon multiplying Americans. The teacher of the country school is one of the greatest factors in this work.

CHAPTER III.

THE SCHOOL HOUSE.

I. SCHOOL ARCHITECTURE.

NOT one-half enough money is expended in the construction of school-houses, and much that is expended is misdirected and the result is that in a land of wealth where costly residences, fine court-houses and penitentiaries, and elegant churches abound the great majority of the school buildings are miserable shanties, barely sufficient to shelter the inmates from the weather, without yards or trees, or anything which makes a home desirable. The school-house is not exactly a home, but it should be just as attractive a place. Our cities, as a rule, it is true, contain fine school-houses and there are, also, some very neat, well-arranged and attractive school-houses in the country, but it is the exception rather than the rule. Four bare walls of wood, stone or brick, with desks and table for the teacher, a rusty stove and rustier walls with a greasy black-board about three by four feet in dimensions, will pretty accurately describe the inside of the majority of country schoolhouses, at least, those in the Central and Western States.

Our free school system is a grand and glorious thing, and much money is spent for the sustenance of schools; yet when we consider the money spent for useless purposes it is but a trifle. The annual expenditure in the United States for sites, buildings, furniture, libraries and apparatus is only a little over ten million dollars. Compare this with the cost of punishing crime, or with the amount annually expended for liquors and tobacco. The people can be taxed to no better purpose, certainly, than that of educating their children. It is a fact that as education of the masses increases, crime and its consequences decreases; consequently it is a good investment, for it is a saving to the country to the amount necessary to punish crime as well as the loss of property consequent upon crime. It is also true that the more money expended by the State for the purpose of maintaining schools the fewer illiterate persons there are. The following statistics, compiled from official sources, will show this:

Iowa, for every one of her population expends $3.60, and one out of every 49 of her population over ten years of age can not read.

Tennessee, for every one of her population expends 55 cents, and one out of every four of her population over ten years of age can not read. It may be objected that as Tennessee has a large Negro population, the comparison is unfair. Take, then, the State of New Jersey instead.

New Jersey, for every one of her population expends $2.37, and one out of every 27 of her population over ten years of age can not read.

Thus you may figure up the statistics of any State and find that the more money expended for schools the less ignorance among the people.

It frequently happens that a sufficient sum of money is appropriated for buildings and apparatus but so misdirected that it fails to answer any good purpose.

Practical teachers are rarely consulted when a country school-house is to be built. I have seen some very costly buildings that were miserable failures as school-houses. One third less money would have built better houses for the purpose, if it had been properly applied. For example, I have one in mind just now which cost a large sum of money. There were two small ante-rooms, so arranged that they were of little practical use, and to conceal the want of symmetry, caused by thus arranging the rooms, a blind window was made between the entries to them. A belfry costing a large sum, and made more for ornament, though not very ornamental, than for use, was placed on the top. An attempt was made to construct a blackboard in the wall, but it was a failure, from want of a little knowledge, and consequently, was never used for that purpose.

It is the duty of teachers, at the risk even of being thought meddlesome, to instruct school boards when new houses are to be built, and see that what money is expended is used to the best purpose. But how can teachers instruct others unless they are themselves instructed in this matter? The question of school architecture is one of great importance, and not enough attention is paid to it by teachers. In the first place, then, teacher, urge a sufficient expenditure, and then see that it is properly applied.

I give here a few suggestions as to how I think country school-houses should be constructed:

1. *Location.* As the distance to be traversed by the pupils must be taken into consideration, not a very wide latitude of choice is allowable in this respect, but when possible, a high ground should be chosen, near a natural forest, and far enough away from the public highway to be free from the noise, dust and danger of passing vehicles. How often do we see these points disregarded. Country school-houses are often "stuck in a mud hole" and so close to the road side that passing vehicles may rub against their sides.

2. *Surroundings.* Land is not excessively dear in this country and there can be no excuse for not having ample grounds in connection with the school-house. There should not in the Western States be less than two acres. In the older States where land is now higher, perhaps a less space may be all that can be expected. The ground should be enclosed with a neat fence, and if not naturally furnished with trees the more hardy kinds of forest trees should be planted, not in straight rows but in groups as they grow naturally, leaving a

large space at a sufficient distance from the house, for a play-ground for ball and such games as require open ground. All out buildings should be at the back of the school-house some distance and screened by trees. I will say nothing of laying off flower beds and planting shrubbery, though intensely desirable, as I fear we are not quite sufficiently civilized for that, especially in the West.

3. *Size.* There is little danger of getting a school-house too large. I have yet to meet with a country school-house too large for the number of pupils. Here comes in the matter of expense, and here is where teachers must fight the parsimony that will crowd a number of children together like cattle in a pen.

A school-house to accommodate 60 pupils should not be less than 32 by 40 feet in dimensions and include a hall and two ante-rooms. This will give ample room for desks, recitation seats, platform and aisles, and desks need not be placed too close to the stove. The ceiling should be at least 10 feet high. For a smaller school the building need not be quite so large, perhaps in some districts not more than 26 by 34 feet.

4. *Plan.* I submit the following plan for a country school-house, which is calculated to seat sixty-two pupils, and give all ample accommodations, hoping it will, at at least, prove suggestive. For convenience in study-ing Geography as well as for other reasons the pupils should be seated facing the north, the door entering at the south and the north a dead wall, windows being on the east and west sides:

60 METHODS OF TEACHING

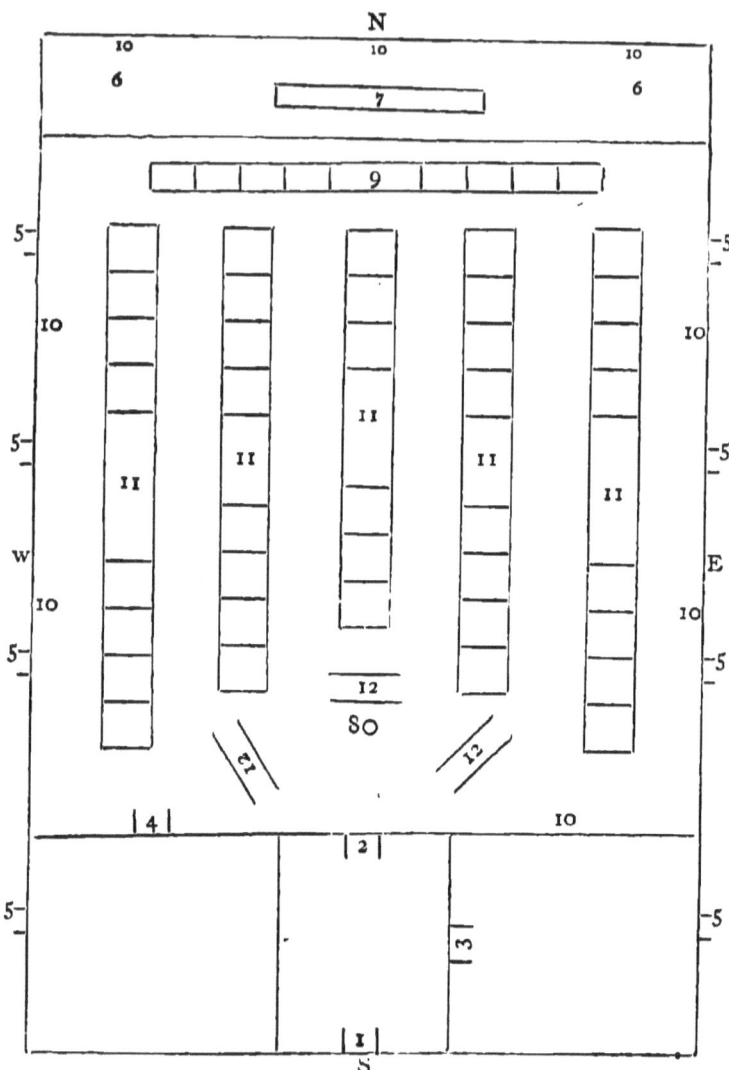

1. Outside Door.
2. Inside Door.
3. Door to Clothes Room.
4. Door to Teacher's Room.
5. Windows.
6. Platform 10 inches.
7. Teacher's Desk.
8. Stove.
9. Recitation Seats.
10. Blackboards.
11. Desks for 62 Pupils.
12. Movable Seats.

The small room on the right of the hall can be used for hanging clothes, keeping dinner baskets, a small supply of fuel, kindlings, &c. The room on the left I have denominated the teacher's room, but may be used for a variety of purposes. A school library may be kept here, also all apparatus when not in use, and if occasion requires it may be used as a recitation room. The stove, it will be observed, is far enough from any pupil's desk and opposite and near to the door, the advantage of which will be seen when we come to speak of ventilation. A large black-board can be made the full width of the room at the north end and facing the school, while smaller black-boards can be made between the windows. The windows are all at the sides, an arrangement better suited to the eyes of the pupils than if facing them. They should be made high so that the light will shine rather down on the pupils. The aisles should be two feet or more in width.

Such a building will cost a little more than such as are usually built, but when once built will last just as long as a more contracted structure and will certainly pay in an educational sense.

5. *Construction and Material.* School-houses may be made of wood, stone, brick or concrete, but of whatever material, they should be well constructed and the material should be of the best quality of the kind. No bungling workmen should have the contract for building.

The great objection to large rooms with high ceilings is that they are inclined to echo and increase sounds. This may be obviated in a great measure by so constructing the floor as to deaden the sound. Architects can accomplish this and it should be a part of the specifications.

Floors should be made of hard wood, the boards being narrow and well joined so as not to warp. The room should be ceiled with boards to a height of three or four feet all around. The windows should have shutters on the outside.

Black-boards should be made in the wall. Perhaps the best is made by mixing lampblack and flour of emery with plaster of Paris and put on as the last coat of plastering, the same as a hard finish.

It would lessen the expense somewhat by setting the roof down lower and making the ceiling arched or higher in the middle than at the sides. Thus at a less expense for material would be gained the same or greater amount of space.

II. APPARATUS.

Many school-houses in this country have not one piece of apparatus, not even a wall map. This is a deplorable state of affairs, and I hope it will not always be thus. Now, I am not going to advocate the purchasing of costly apparatus. There is no need of it; but there are a few articles which no school board should neglect to furnish. Among these are a good set of wall maps, a small globe, an unabridged dictionary, and charts for teaching penmanship and primary reading. Besides these there might be an encyclopedia of general information, a tellurian to illustrate mathematical geography, a set of mathematical blocks, set of alphabet blocks, a numeral frame, a number of small rulers with scale of inches marked, and a yard stick. Some of these may be easily made by the teacher.

According to Webster's definition of apparatus, viz: "Things provided as means to some end," it will not be improper to include a library as among the apparatus of a school. I have already mentioned two works of reference, but there are many books not only valuable for reference but for the use of the children and youth of our country schools. It seems to me that with a school-house as I have here described, a library should be started. I hope that the day is not far distant when each country school-house will be constructed on some similar plan to the one described, and in the teacher's room there will be a book case well filled with reading matter and works of reference suitable to the young and for the benefit of the teacher. Such a library can be kept under lock and key and the teacher constituted a librarian, books only to be had during session of the school. The legislature of Ohio once voted a school library to be kept in each district, and the books to be exchanged periodically. It was only a few years until the books were scattered and most of them lost, and finally what was left were gathered up and sold. It does seem to me that such a state of affairs does not argue a very highly civilized state of society. If men took that interest in the education of their children which they should take, such would not be the case. Now, I do think that if each district would furnish its own library, and school boards would see to it that teachers did their duty as librarians (and if teachers were alive to their work they would need but little watching), a great revolution in the state of society might be accomplished in a few years. Certain books, such as are not used for reference, might be exchanged from one district to another at certain intervals, thus keeping up new interest. The schoolhouse should be the literary center of the rural community. These libraries would be excellent helps to literary societies which could be held at the schoolhouse during winter evenings.

Public exhibitions, festivals, etc., might be given, and the proceeds devoted to purchasing a library for the school. Other apparatus might be procured in a similar manner.

III. VENTILATION.

I shall not occupy space in speaking of the evils of badly ventilated rooms. Every person of intelligence knows the advantages of ventilation.

A room is well ventilated when there is a free access of fresh air and a free exit for the foul air, and when no one is exposed to cold draughts. The bad effects from draughts are even greater evils than breathing impure air. The majority, in fact nearly all, country school-houses are so constructed that they can not be ventilated without exposing pupils to cold draughts of air. If a window is raised at the bottom the cold air rushes in and strikes those sitting near it, and if it is lowered from the top the cold air falls down on the heads of the inmates.

Air that has been inhaled by the lungs contains carbonic acid gas, as well as organic matters resulting from the waste of animal tissue. This carbonic acid is heavier than common air when cold, but when warmed it is lighter than common cool air. The consequence is that when exhaled from the lungs it rises, but gradually descends as it becomes cooled If an opening is made near the top of the room it will pass out readily, provided there is a sufficient opening at the bottom to admit a corresponding amount of fresh air. If there is no admission of cool air from below and an opening made at the top there will be two currents established side by side, one of cold air coming in and the other of warm, foul air passing out. The cold air will fall down to the bottom of the room and force the warmer air up. An interesting experiment may be performed by the teacher to illustrate this principle of ventilation. When a room which contains a fire has been closed for some time, let the door be opened for the space of an inch or more and hold a lighted candle opposite the crack. If it is held near the top the flame will be blown outward; if near the bottom it will be blown inward, and if near the middle it will remain steady, showing plainly the direction of the currents of air.

As a simple and effective means of ventilating a school-room, I would recommend the following: Make a wooden spout, say six inches or more in diameter, to pass from beneath the stove to the outside of the building, under the floor. An opening is to be made in the floor under the stove. At the end of the room farthest from the stove make a similar spout to extend from the floor to the roof, with openings at the top and bottom and in the middle, with slides to shut when necessary. Now, when a fire is made the air around the stove becomes heated, and rising, circulates through the room and passes out at the openings in the upright spout. A fresh supply of cold air is drawn through the tube under the floor and in turn becomes heated and circulates through the room. The windows and doors may be shut perfectly tight, and yet there will be good ventilation.

Heat is conducted from a stove through a room in two ways—by convection and by radiation. By the former is meant that the air in immediate contact with the stove becomes heated, and rising, its place is supplied by cool air, which goes through the same process. By radiation is meant that heat is thrown off from the stove in direct rays, the same as light from a lamp. To prevent this heating by radiation some device must be applied, because those sitting near the stove get too warm, while those at a distance may suffer with cold. A piece of sheet-iron or tin should be placed so as to surround the stove on all sides, except top and bottom, at the distance of four or five inches. The stove should always stand near the door of the room to receive the cool air when the door is opened. A room ventilated and warmed as above described will not be an unhealthful place for human beings.

But what are you going to do, teacher, if you are obliged to teach in a room not properly ventilated? Rather than open a window and expose some pupil to a draught, which will be the case in most houses, open doors and windows wide at each recess and noon and allow a thorough change of air. When pupils are in motion the draughts will not hurt them. Or a window may be opened and the opening screened by a board so as to prevent a direct draught. If the stove is near the door, as it should be, open the door a little way to admit air, provided the pupils are not so seated that the air will strike them.

An attention to these matters will often prevent cases of colds which might result in disease producing death. A close, ill-ventilated room will also make restless pupils, and government will be more difficult in such a room. The teacher is responsible in great measure for the health and comfort of his pupils.

PART II—METHODS OF TEACHING.

CHAPTER I.

READING.

To be a good reader is a most desirable accomplishment. As reading is taught in our ungraded schools we can not say it is a success. The hesitation and drawl of too many school boys and the sing-song tone of, alas, too many ministers are simply abominable. Yet much time is spent in all our schools in the acquisition of this art. The results should be more satisfactory.

To make a good reader it requires, first, a knowledge of the principles of elocution; second, much practice.

In order to teach the principles of elocution, the teacher himself should have a knowledge of them. Too many teachers are wofully deficient in this respect. It must be remembered that a strict observance of the rules for articulation, inflection, accent and emphasis, pitch, gesture, etc., will not make a good reader or speaker. He should enter into the spirit and meaning of the author. He must understand and *feel* what he reads or speaks. The rules of elocution have many exceptions; so much so that they seem arbitrary. The best orators are children and Indians, because they speak the language of nature, and are not drilled into artificial modes of expression by unnatural customs.

The teacher should endeavor to improve himself in this noble art. He should practice much, reading aloud and declaiming, at the same time studying the principles of elocution, as found in our School Readers. He should first try to find out his own faults and set himself to remedy them. If he finds he does not articulate well, he should practice on this branch until he has improved his enunciation. In the same manner let him correct, by drilling himself, any other faults of expression he may possess. Let the country teacher, after his pupils have gone home in the evening, read and declaim to the empty seats for half an hour each day the lessons in the Readers. The time thus spent will repay him many fold. It will elevate him not only among teachers, but among all classes.

It is expected of a teacher, above all others, that he should possess the art of expressing himself. The American people are a nation of readers, but there are comparatively few good readers among them. It is true that a republic is the best calculated to develop oratory, and we have many of the greatest orators in the world, yet we should have more of them and more who should be above mediocrity in this respect. It is the duty of the country teacher to manufacture many of the future orators of America. Let him fit himself by careful study and constant drill for this purpose.

Now that the country teacher is obliged to teach

everything from A B C to Algebra, it is not to be supposed he will have the time to devote to the subject of reading which the teacher of a graded school can have, but what time he has should be economized and profitably used. The time devoted to each class, of course, will vary with the number of branches taught in the school, the number of pupils, and, perhaps, with other circumstances. For example, in some schools, will be found Algebra, Physiology, History, and, perhaps, two grades each of Grammar and Geography, while in other schools there may be neither of the first three, and only one class each in the two latter. The time, therefore, must vary with circumstances. (See p. 35.)

Teaching Beginners to Read.

There are various methods in vogue for teaching beginners to read. Each one has its advocates, who strenuously hold to their particular methods, just as the different schools of medicine or the different denominations of religious believers hold to their respective dogmas. Now, I do not wish to be behind the times, and advise my readers to follow a method which the present age has voted down, but I will say that I have some serious objections to following exclusively any method which has yet been invented. There are some methods, as the various phonic methods, which in *theory* seem to be just the thing, and the enthusiastic young teacher will likely be carried away by the specious arguments used in their favor by some of our educators, who, having watched them in the quiet of their study rooms, and never having given them a practical test in the school-room, are prepared to denounce any one as an old fogy or an ignoramus who will not at once fall in love with them. I will say here that I have personal knowledge of at least one prominent educator who is an ardent advocate of what he calls the phonetic or normal method, and who has never taught a class of children in his life.

The different methods may be enumerated as follows: The *Alphabetic Method*, the *Word or Webb Method*, the *Phonic Method*. Of the latter there are several varieties.

The *Alphabetic Method* is the one by which the most of us perhaps were taught and the one which is in use in the greater number of country schools to-day. It needs no explanation, being simply the teaching of the names of the letters of the alphabet and the combining of them into words. The objection made to it is that it teaches the names of the letters only and not their powers and sounds, and that it is synthetic rather than analytic.

The *Word or Webb Method* has many advocates. By this method the learner is taught first a number of words as wholes. Objects or pictures of objects are shown to the pupils and they are taught to call the words which represent them at sight. Words are combined in sentences and the child is thus taught to read before he knows a single letter. The letters are then, it is claimed, learned very readily by separating the words into their component letters. The advantages claimed for this method over the former are that it is analytic rather than synthetic, and that it can be made much more interesting to children, words representing ideas being more easily grasped as wholes than letters, which are but arbitrary signs.

The *Phonic Method* claims superiority over the others from the fact that as our alphabet contains only twenty-six letters to represent about forty sounds, by teaching the sounds of the letters rather than their names, the many difficulties of pronouncing our language are obviated. As before stated there are several varieties of the Phonic Method. Some have tried to overcome the difficulties by having the sounds of the letters indicated by marks over or under them, as they are in the dictionary. Others have the primers printed representing the different sounds by different styles of type, and others still by using different characters for each sound.

It will be useless to discuss here these different methods. I have only briefly described them that the teacher may not be ignorant of them, and will say that if circumstances permit it will be well for the teacher to try the new methods and thus be able to decide for himself. I will only here state a few facts concerning the matter of teaching beginners in country schools, and then describe the method I have used with the greatest success.

1. A great many children learn the alphabet, and some to spell a little, before they are sent to school.

2. The country teacher will find in many schools only one, or at most only two or three pupils, who can not read quite well in the First Reader.

3. Children love to put things together, to build up, as well as they love to take things apart or tear

down. Both synthesis and analysis should be used in teaching.

4. Children learn almost unconsciously the sounds of the letters by naming the letters in familiar words and hearing the words pronounced. Thus rarely a child needs be told twice that c-a-t spells *cat*, although the sounds of the letters, as heard in the word, are not the same as the names of the letters. The converse is true that even advanced pupils will hesitate about pronouncing a word which is unfamiliar to them, even though it be a word of very easy construction.

5. It is a rather difficult matter to get a child to give the sound of a letter alone. In pronouncing words he gives the sounds of the letters combined, but if you attempt to get a child to give, say the short sound of *a* in *căt*, you will find he does not seem to comprehend what you mean, and he will hesitate to repeat the sound after the teacher.

6. The fact is, the child has been accustomed from infancy to pronouncing words, i. e. giving the sounds of letters combined in such a way that they represent ideas which he has previously acquired, and sounds alone and letters alone represent to his mind no ideas at all. This is why it is a difficult matter to teach the alphabet or its sounds.

From the above facts and from my own experience I have found the following method, which may be termed the "Eclectic Method,"* the most applicable in a country school:

---

* See Wickersham's Methods of Instruction.

If no suitable books or charts are at hand, I first show the class a simple object, as a box, asking its name. Then I show them a picture of a box in a book, or draw its picture on the black-board. Then I print the word box on the board. Next I teach the difference between an object, the picture of an object and a word representing the object. Then I tell them the word is made up of letters, asking them how many, and naming for them each letter, requiring them to repeat them after me. Then the word is pronounced slowly, so as to somewhat isolate each sound. Next I take a word having the same letters, or part of them, and drill in the same manner. The word *ox* would appropriately follow *box*, or *at* follow *cat*. A few letters are learned at a time; they are learned by using them, and their powers are learned at the same time. I proceed thus until all the letters are learned by their *use* in words familiar and easy of pronunciation. As soon as a few words are learned I combine them into sentences, and the pupils read them until they are quite familiar with them. The books may be used sometimes when they contain pictures and words which are applicable. Charts containing pictures and easy words will be found quite convenient. When a letter is learned by the pupil he may be shown a printed page and exercised in finding out the letter from among others. Blocks with the letters printed on them are very useful. With them words can be put together and taken apart.

An ingenious teacher will find many ways of varying the lessons and making them interesting. Pupils, while learning to read, may be taught some ideas of number. This will vary the exercises and will interest the pupils. They may be required to count the letters in a word, the words in a sentence, the windows in the room or the number of panes in the windows, etc. There are some letters so nearly alike in form that pupils sometimes find it difficult to distinguish between them, for instance b and d and p and q. The teacher may show them how they are made, that is with a straight line and a curve either at top, bottom, right or left sides. The pupil should be required to form the letters with pencil or chalk. This will give employment and help fix the forms of the letters in their minds.

As soon as the letters are learned, exercise should be given in pronouncing words, and continued until they can call a great number of easy and familiar words at sight. Words having a similarity of sound, provided they are simple and convey ideas which the pupil is already familiar with, may be arranged in columns and pronounced first down the column and then across the page. In this way words are learned by their resemblance to each other, and a test is made by pronouncing across the columns.

FIRST READER.

As soon as the child has learned to call a number of words readily at sight, attention should be paid to the following points:

1. *Secure Distinct Articulation.*

The teacher should see that the child opens his

mouth properly and articulates every sound fully and clearly. Never allow a word to pass until you are satisfied the pupil has articulated it as distinctly as you think it possible for him to do. There are defects of the vocal organs which may be remedied in great measure by practice, but it is not expected that a teacher should devote the time necessary to cure stammering and such like defects. This should be done at home or in schools specially for that purpose. Words of the lesson difficult of pronunciation may be printed on the black-board, and the class pronounce in rotation or occasionally in concert. Let the pupils spell the difficult words from the book and pronounce them. Then let the teacher pronounce them and the pupils spell them without looking on the book. Then let them read to a period, or a paragraph.

2. *Secure Natural Tones and Delivery.*

Do not let them drawl out their words. Right here many bad readers are made if attention is not paid to this point. This drawling habit will go with them through life. Read the sentence for them and have them read it as they would talk it. Teach them the use of the period and interrogation point. Other marks may be deferred for the present.

3. *See that Pupils take a Proper Position.*

The posture, whether sitting or standing, should be erect, with shoulders thrown back. Do not allow pupils to lean on anything. This is a very bad habit and pupils need to be corrected frequently for it. If it is not corrected here the habit of lounging will go with them through life. This is one of the greatest faults with which a country teacher has to contend. Pupils should stand with their heels nearly together and toes apart, about at an angle of forty-five degrees. For a rest and change one foot may be thrown out so that the heel comes opposite the instep of the other foot. They may change weight of body from one foot to the other as often as necessary to prevent weariness.

4. *Cultivate Perception and Language.*

Ask questions upon the subject matter of the lessons. Show them a picture and ask them to point out the objects. Print an easy sentence on the blackboard, leaving a word to be supplied by the pupil. This will do for an occasional exercise.

5. *Prepare for the Next Lesson.*

Pronounce difficult words. They may be placed upon the board. Require pupils to print on their slates a certain number of words of the next lesson. This will give them occupation at their seats. Always give a certain number of words to print and let it be a less number than is given at the head of the lesson, telling them to select what they think the hardest words. In this way they exercise their judgment, and it pleases them to be allowed to select the words.

SECOND READER.

Continue the methods used in the First Reader, if

necessary, to secure the points indicated under that head.

You may ask more difficult questions upon the subject matter of the lesson. Teach the use of the comma and semicolon. Give an occasional concert drill, something after this manner:

The teacher reads a sentence, if it be a short one, or a part of a sentence, if it be too long, and the class reads after him. The signal for them to begin, a tap of the pencil. Repeat until all can begin and end at the same instant. In this way the fast readers are checked and the slow ones hurried up. Get them to imitate your tones and expression as nearly as possible. Select the most difficult parts of the lesson to be read in this way. You can vary the exercise by asking questions about the punctuation marks or about the subject matter of what is read.

Pay more attention to the spelling of the words at the head of the lesson. A greater number should be assigned to copy on slates than in the First Reader. Words that are missed by all the class may be printed on the blackboard and spelled in concert by the class.

Teach emphasis and inflection by having them imitate your reading.

THIRD READER.

Continue exercises given in Second Reader, making them more difficult. Teach the use of italic letters, the apostrophe when it is used in contracting words, and the use of capital letters. Tell them that the name of every person or place, the names of the days of the week, and names of the months, the words I and O, and the first word after every period always begin with a capital letter. The other rules for the use of capitals may be omitted for the present. Fix these points by frequent drills. It is a good exercise to write a sentence occasionally on the board, omitting capitals where they should belong and placing them where they should not, and have the class correct it. Exercises in correcting false spelling may also be given.

The pupil now should be taught, if possible, to write instead of print the spelling lists. Most pupils reading in the Third Reader are able to form the script letters, and wherever they can they should be required to do so.

Give the meaning of the more difficult words in the next lesson. First ask the class to define the words; if no one can give the meaning, give it yourself, and tell them you will ask them at the next recitation. You can easily overdo this matter of defining words. It is best to talk to the class in a familiar way about the words, giving their meaning by their use in easy sentences. It is better even that they should pass some words which they do not know, rather than too great a tax be put upon their minds or too much time consumed by the teacher. (See p. 84.)

Give exercises in articulation something after this manner: A word, as *night*, is written on the blackboard, and the teacher asks the class to pronounce it. Then the teacher asks how many letters in the word, then spells it by sound, requiring the class to repeat the sounds after him, then asking them how many sounds in the word, what letters are silent, etc.

Exercises for articulation should always be real words, not mere combinations of letters to represent certain sounds. I think it an error to drill children in pronouncing such combinations as *fwoi, dofst, tifst,* etc. For further examples of this kind see McGuffey's Third Reader, p. 9.

FOURTH READER.

Continue the exercises given in Third Reader where necessary.

Give more frequent drills on emphasis and inflection. Teach the use of inflection marks, quotation marks and hyphen. Have class criticise each others' reading. It is a good exercise occasionally to allow the class to remain at their desks and call out one at a time to step upon the rostrum and read a paragraph or two, the others criticising his position, tone and expression, etc.

One or more words may be assigned to each pupil to spell and define from memory at the next recitation. The teacher may add to the words at the head of the lesson; others, requesting the pupils to go to the Dictionary for their meaning. Teach how to find words in the Dictionary. Pupils may be required to write the word and its definition on the slate. Occasionally write a sentence on the board, containing proper names, common abbreviations, contractions of words, etc., and require pupils to copy on slates. Make this an exercise in penmanship. Give the most common rules for the use of capitals and frequent drills to fix them.

As members of the Fourth Reader class usually have other studies, not so much time need be spent writing the spelling lists as in the Third Reader.

ADVANCED READING.

Under this head comes Fifth and Sixth Readers as usually found in common schools. Continue methods used in Fourth Reader, and practice frequently upon the exercises given under the rules of elocution in the books. Call the attention of the class to the rules which should govern them in the piece to be read. Passages which illustrate particular rules in the next lesson should be read and commented upon by the teacher as a preliminary drill. Explain geographical and historical points in the lesson. Point out the beauties and excellencies of authors, and tell anything regarding their lives which you know and would be interesting to the class. Instruction may be given upon versification so far as pointing out the kinds of poetic feet, kinds of verse and poetic license. These matters to be governed by the powers of your pupils, the time allotted you, and your own qualifications. (See page 35.)

GENERAL OBSERVATIONS.

The teacher should, in teaching reading, hold constantly in mind two points, viz: 1st. To secure a proper oral expression of written or printed composition; 2d. To develop and increase the power of grasping thought. The first point is to be secured by constant drill and practice in the management of the voice. In the cultivation of the voice four points are to be considered, *Quantity, Quality, Compass* and *Movement*.

Emphasis, Force, Stress, Slur and *Accent* are all modifications of *Quantity*. These parts should be taught from the First Reader up, mainly in primary classes by imitation of the teacher. The greatest failing in schools comes under this head. One half of the pupils in all our schools do not read sufficiently loud and strong. Teachers should take particular pains to remedy this by constant effort from the beginning of the pupil's school life. The teacher should stand at a distance from the pupils and require them to read loud enough to be heard in all parts of the room. Give frequent exercise in pronouncing the vowel sounds, words and sentences, with different degrees of force.

The most difficult part of vocal culture, perhaps, is *Quality* of the voice. In order to read in a proper tone the reader must place himself in the position of the author and enter into his very soul, that he may express his feelings. The pupil must understand the nature of the sentiment before he can give the proper tone. Much may be learned by imitating the teacher, especially with very young pupils.

Nothing but careful training can give the proper *pitch* and *inflection* of the voice, and ability to read well depends greatly upon this power. Certain vowel sounds, as *a* or *o*, or words as *do, ra*, may be given in different keys until the class is able to pitch their voices upon any key within their *compass*. Drills in inflection may be given by arranging a series of words and sentences in the form of questions and answers, requiring one portion of the class to give the question and the other the answer.

Under the head of *Movement* come *Rate* and *Pause*. Many pupils habitually read too fast, while others are too slow. Concert reading, as an occasional practice, is good to regulate this matter. The marks of punctuation, of course, are not to be disregarded, but there are other pauses required by the sense, and the pupil must understand what he is reading or he can not give them. Paragraphs may be selected by the teacher and the class drilled in reading them with reference to rate and pause.

The Teacher Should Endeavor to Develop the Power of Grasping Thought.

A good reader is able to grapple with a whole sentence almost at a glance and take in its full purport. This part of mental training is very much neglected everywhere. But few persons, comparatively, know how to read a book so as to get at the substance of the discourse. We must know how, as it were, to swoop down upon a mass of words and bear away the ideas expressed. With many writers the words are so many and the ideas are so few and so well concealed that it requires the penetrating eye of a hawk and the power of a magnet to discover and drag out the gems of truth from the mass of rubbish. The teacher can do much by asking numerous questions upon the subject matter of what is read. The questions should be asked in various ways, so as to draw out the full meaning of the author. As an example of the method of asking questions to young beginners, I give the following:

The trees lift up their green heads in the bright light of spring.
Question. What lift up their green heads?
Answer. The trees.
Q. Where do they lift up their green heads?
A. In the bright light of spring.
Q. What kind of heads do they lift up?
A. Green heads.
Q. What kind of light is spoken of?
A. Bright light.
Q. Light of what?
A. Light of spring.

Single sentences may be taken in this way and analyzed until the pupils see the full force of what they have read. Questions of an entirely different character should also be given on the entire lesson, questions which should be answered in the pupil's own language. Such questions will not only test the fact of their understanding of the lesson, but develop their power of expression and cultivate language. Examples of such questions are given in most readers.

It should not be expected of pupils that they understand absolutely everything they read. There are many words which they may have an idea of, yet not a complete one, and many expressions which they can not see the full force and meaning; but these things will be learned as they grow older. Again, a pupil may have a pretty good idea of the meaning of a word, yet not be able to express his meaning in words. This is the case with all of us, especially with many familiar words which we use every day. To test this, ask your pupils to give a definition of stove, chair, table, etc. Try yourself to give a definition of these words. I venture to assert that not one teacher out of a thousand can give a complete definition of these words. (See page 79.)

Our text-books are not always just as they should be. Many of the lessons for young children are too far above their comprehension.

Many teachers assert that pupils should be assigned very short reading lessons, and they should be read over and over again until they are thoroughly understood and can be read with a great degree of perfection. This, I think, is a mistake. It is a hobby I used to ride myself, but I found it not a safe one, from this fact, children soon tire of one thing, and a piece read over so many times becomes almost disgusting, and less interest will be taken and consequently less progress made. Our reading books should be twice as large and twice as many. But an item of expense here comes in which is quite an objection. If we could only have many more lessons, each one illustrating the same points in elocution, but in which the matter is different and consequently always something new and interesting, I think much greater progress would be made. The rule will apply all the way from beginners up. As soon as a child has learned to call a dozen words at sight, these words should be arranged in as many sentences as possible, each sentence expressing a new thought or expressing it in a new way.

All children love stories. The juvenile papers and magazines and nursery books all have a great influence in teaching children and youth to read. How much more progress would be made if they read them under the eye of a teacher than by themselves. But as we must accept our text-books as they are, for the present at least, what can the country teacher do in this case? I have a plan to propose:

In many schools reading classes are small, sometimes not more than two or three, and owing to the irregular attendance in country schools, there will be many days when some one or more of the classes in reading will have but two or three pupils. In such cases assign a lesson from a newspaper, a Sunday-school paper, a juvenile magazine, or any book in which you may find stories or descriptive sketches suited to the wants of your particular class. The pupils can take the paper or book in turn and read the piece over, or copy certain parts of it on their slates, and when recitation comes they may look on the same book, or, each one having copied his own part, pay strict attention to the others reading their parts, and criticisms may be made by the class. The teacher may take a story from a newspaper and cut into sections, giving each one a section, and require it copied on slates and read from the slate at recitation. This can be made an exercise in spelling, capitals, punctuation and penmanship.

Country teachers might club together and write or select from books or papers pieces suited to all their classes and have them printed in their county paper. A number of copies of the paper may be taken by the club and each teacher use them in turn. If they are taken care of they may be used for many schools. Country editors can easily be induced to print such matter if the object is explained to them; in fact, if a club is formed and a number of copies taken it will be to their advantage to do so. Other matter in these papers, such as marriage and death notices, local news, advertisements, etc., may be used in advanced classes, as an occasionel variation from the monotony of the text-book. In this, as in other parts of teaching, the teacher should bend every faculty to his work. (See p. 206.)

In all his reading, which should embrace a wide scope, he should be on the lookout for whatever may benefit his classes. Little stories and sketches are found almost every day by a general reader, and the teacher should try to secure and preserve them for future use.

Occasional reading lessons from the geographies, grammars, arithmetics and histories may be given to vary the exercises. The Constitution of the United States, the Declaration of Independence, Articles of Confederation, etc., to be found in all school histories, should be read one or more times during a term by advanced classes.

CHAPTER II.

SPELLING AND DEFINING.

The orthography of the English language is difficult. The majority of the words are not phonetic, and the rules for spelling have too many exceptions to be of much utility.

We learn to spell both by the eye and by the ear. Both written and oral spelling exercises should be employed. We hear a word spelled and remember the order of the letters, or we con the words over, repeating the letters, and thus fix their order in our minds. Thus we learn by the ear. We see a word written or printed and observe the order and position of the letters as we would the objects in a picture, and they become fixed in our memory, and thus we learn by the eye. Writing spelling has the advantage of giving employment to pupils who would otherwise, perhaps, be in mischief. It also affords training to the hand and is an aid in penmanship.

In addition to the spelling exercises in connection with the reading lessons, daily drills in spelling, defining, capitalization, punctuation and abbreviations should be given, the entire school, from the Second Reader up, participating.

I have found it best to classify the school into two

general classes, a primary and an advanced. Each of these classes may be divided into two sections that the exercises may be graded to their capacities. The different sections may be assigned different parts of the same lesson, but it can be so managed that there need be but one recitation for each class. Not less than fifteen minutes should be devoted to each recitation.

For an advanced class I give a lesson something as follows: Ten or more words are selected and written upon the black-board in the morning, in as neat and plain a manner as possible, the letters made according to the Spencerian System. I can best illustrate this by giving a model lesson:

1. curriculum
2. Joseph Ray, M. D.
3. daguerreotype
4. autumnal
5. Wm. H. McGuffey, LL. D.
6. stationary
7. stationery
8. Springfield, Ill.
9. Hon. E. S. Sampson, M. C.
10. Marion Co. Democrat

It must be explained to the pupils that words in these lessons are to be written just as they would appear in the middle of a sentence. I have given above rather more words, which should be capitalized, and more abbreviations than I would in an ordinary lesson. Perhaps one or two such examples would be sufficient in each lesson. It will be seen by the above that capitalization, punctuation and abbreviations are taught in a natural manner.

This lesson may remain upon the board until within an hour of the time of recitation, which should be near the close of the day. During this time the class should be required to copy it on their slates one or more times. The most backward spellers, and those inclined to be idle, may be required to copy it oftener than the good spellers or those who are diligent. One or more words may be marked and arranged as a lesson in defining, the pupil to find the meaning in the dictionary. The modes of conducting the recitation may be various. The words are erased or, what is better, covered with a shawl, map or newspaper, before the hour of recitation. The teacher, having reserved a slate containing a copy of the lesson, requires the lessons to be erased from all other slates. He then pronounces the words and the pupils write them on their slates. Slates may be exchanged and the pupils criticise each other's work, or each one retain his own slate and mark the misspelled words as the teacher gives the correct spelling. The words may then be spelled orally, the slates being turned down on the desks. All words missed should be written again correctly by the pupils. Words missed by the majority of the class should be taken down by the teacher and used for future lessons. The covering may be removed from the lesson on the board and the pupils correct their slates from that.

As an occasional exercise, say once a week, the class may be provided with pens and ink and slips of paper to write their lessons. The lessons being dated and signed by the pupil, both sides may be used, and they may be kept as a record of the pupil's progress in spelling and penmanship. There are blank books provided for this purpose which are very convenient and cheap.

These written spelling lessons may be varied in many ways. Occasionally, sentences should be given. The dictation exercises given in spelling books are very convenient. The lessons need not always be written. Oral spelling should not be neglected. As spelling books are common in most country schools the teacher may make use of them in various ways. Avoid a routine plan of teaching. Study new methods of conducting spelling drills. There is nothing like variety here to keep up an interest. The old-fashioned custom of having a spelling match every Friday is not a bad one. The ingenious teacher of to-day will, however, find many ways of varying the old plan. A good method in oral spelling is to have the class numbered and their numbers written upon the black-board. The teacher then, with book in one hand and pointer in the other, pronounces a word and points to a certain number. The pupil corresponding to that number spells the word. If he misses a mark is made under his number and the word passed to another. By jumping rapidly from one number to another promiscuously, the pupils are compelled to pay close attention. The number of marks, then, will show the number of words missed by each pupil. Another plan is to have each one of the class have slate and pencil in hand, and whenever a pupil misses let him write the word on the slate. Occasionally, words may be written on the board falsely spelled and pupils be required to write the spelling correctly on slates.

In a written lesson, as given above, the teacher may define the words as he gives them out, sometimes by giving the definition as in the dictionary, or by giving a sentence containing the word, and make such remarks about the origin, etc., of words or terms as he may think proper. Much interesting information may be conveyed in this manner which will not be lost on many of the pupils. He should avoid, however, consuming much time in this manner. (See p. 79.)

Primary classes may receive lessons similar to the above but limited to their capacities. Many will not be able to write with sufficient rapidity to write from dictation, but lessons may be placed on the board occasionally and copied by the class and then recited orally. Lessons from the spelling-book may be assigned and copied on slates as a preparation and recited orally. Occasionally a class may be required to form their own lesson in the following manner: Tell them, each one, to write ten names of objects they saw on the road to school, or objects in the schoolroom, or things used in the kitchen, shop, etc. The slates are then collected and the words given out by the teacher. No two pupils will have exactly the same list of words. Perhaps out of the whole number there will be some words which the majority of the class will miss. In this case a list should be made of such words to be used in future recitations. Easy abbreviations and contractions, such as *Dr.*, *Mr.*, *can't*, *couldn't*, etc., may be given primary pupils. It is best to exhibit them in sentences showing their use and meaning. The instruction in regard to use of capitals, punctuation, etc., given in reading classes should be repeated in spelling classes. When a class is divided into sections the lesson may be written all together, and words designed for the advanced section designated by a mark, such as a line drawn under them or by inclosing them in a parenthesis.

I would impress upon the teacher the following considerations:

1. Teach such words first which the pupil will be apt to use first in writing a familiar letter or in reading ordinary composition.

2. Constant reviews are necessary to fix certain hard words in the memory, therefore, all words which are frequently misspelled should be made the subjects of future lessons, and words which are very easy should not occupy the time of the pupils.

3. Too many of the words found in spelling-books are to be found nowhere else outside of medical, law or other technical works, and pupils should not be required to study them until necessity for their use demands it. A common newspaper is one of the best places from which to select words for spelling lessons.

4. In giving out words to be spelled the teachers should pronounce them distinctly and properly, as he would were he reading a composition containing them. He should never pronounce the word wrong to assist the pupil in spelling it. In oral spelling the pupil should be required to pronounce the word before spelling it, and in spelling to pronounce each syllable as he spells it.

5. In assigning a lesson call attention to one or more of the difficult words, telling the pupils such words they will very likely miss unless they study them particularly. I have pursued this plan with somewhat surprising results. If I found a very difficult word I remarked, on assigning the lesson, that I did not think any one would be able to spell that word to-morrow. I could see among several pupils a look of incredulity, as much as to say, "I am not going to miss it," and the consequence was that the particular word was generally spelled by even the dullest in the class.

6. It will not be amiss to teach something of spelling along with other branches. New words occurring in arithmetic, grammar and history may be spelled by the pupils.

7. It may have been noticed by many teachers that those who spell well orally do not always spell correctly when writing. I have seen pupils who could spell any word in the spelling-book if pronounced to them, yet if they were to write a letter to a friend would misspell ten per cent. of the words. This is owing, in a great measure, to carelessness. The hand being occupied in forming the letters, and the mind in composing, one is too apt to neglect the spelling of the words. This fault will be found more especially with those who have never been accustomed to practicing writing spelling. Many persons habitually misspell in writing certain very easy words. This is done by mere "slips of the pen," and is a result of want of attention. The teacher should take particular care to impress upon his pupils the importance of close

attention to this matter. It is a good exercise to occasionally dictate a long sentence composed of easy words and have the class write it as rapidly as possible and then correct the errors, not only in spelling, but in punctuation and capitalization. A short poem or hymn may be committed to memory or one chosen which is already familiar to the pupils, as "Mary's Lamb," "The Little Star," etc., and the pupils be required to copy it from memory and afterwards correct their mistakes from the book. The Lord's Prayer, passages from the Bible, or any short piece of composition the pupil is able to write from memory or can easily commit, may be used in this way. Each pupil may have a different piece and they may be allowed to exchange slates and criticise each other's work. The teacher may look over this work when corrected and point out such errors as may still be found. Beautiful lines of poetry or short, elegant extracts or quotations may be written on the board and committed to memory, and in a day or two afterwards reproduced by the pupils on their slates. Such exercise may be given, say once in two weeks, or monthly.

8. Frequent exercises should be given in addressing letters. The teacher may draw the outline of an envelope on the board and write an address in the proper place, showing where to begin the name, post-office, county and state, and where to place the stamp, and require pupils to draw and address a similar one on their slates, allowing each one to use the name and address of one of their friends.

9. Difficult words may be sometimes spelled in concert by the class after the teacher, or written in

prominent characters on the black-board and allowed to remain several days.

10. The teacher may call attention to some of the most important rules for spelling and syllabication. Very few pupils will, however, learn to spell by rules. Call attention frequently to the diacritical marks used in dictionaries and spelling books. Give drills in spelling by sound. Call attention to words commonly mispronounced and misspelled, and words having more than one authorized pronunciation or spelling. The dictionary should be in every school-room, one copy at least, and frequently referred to by both teacher and pupil.

11. Says Wickersham, "Words are the winged messengers that convey information from one mind and heart to another. All knowledge must be labeled with words or it can find no place in the cabinet of memory." I need not add that it is of exceeding importance that pupils understand the meaning of words which they may find in their daily reading or hear in daily conversation. Many words are learned by a sort of unconscious intuition. Children pick up almost daily and use new words which they hear in conversation or find in their reading. They learn their meaning by their connection. The proper place, then, for the main study of words is in a reading class, but as it will not do to crowd too many things on the pupil's attention at one time the subject may profitably occupy a part of the attention of a spelling class. In fact, attention to the meaning of words should be given in every recitation on whatever subject.

The teacher, in defining words for his pupils, should,

whenever possible, make the meaning plain by showing the object, action or quality which the words represent. For example, the word *calyx* may be explained by showing that part of a flower, the word *diameter* by drawing a circle with a line drawn through the center, also by exhibiting a block, box or ball and explaining that it means the distance through from one side or end to the other; the word *compress* by squeezing in the hand a handkerchief, a rubber ball or a sponge; the words *transparent* and *opaque*, by pointing to the panes of glass in the window and to the walls of the house.

The definitions sometimes given in the dictionary and in reading books are as difficult of comprehension as the words themselves. In this case the teacher should give sentences which make clear the meaning.

A slight knowledge of Latin and Greek will aid much in defining words, but it is not to be expected that pupils in a country school can make use of this knowledge. But it will be of great value to the teacher in studying words. He can, however, teach the meaning of a few prefixes and suffixes and show how they help make words, as *ad*, *ex*, *in*, *sub*, *ion*, *con*, *de*, *re*, etc., and their use in such words as *aspect*, *inspect*, *expect*, *suspect*, *respect*, *conspectus*, *suspicion*, etc.

12. It will not be out of place here to mention that a small printing press is a valuable aid to good spelling and punctuation. Such presses with outfits can be had now for the small sum of five dollars. The teacher may have such a press and permit pupils to use it. He may so interest boys in the art that their

parents will be constrained to procure a press for them. The teacher will find a printing press of value to him for many purposes not necessary to mention here.

CHAPTER III.

ARITHMETIC.

The idea of number is developed early in life. The study of arithmetic may be begun quite early but should not be pushed too rapidly. It is not the most important branch taught in our schools. Many teachers devote too much time to this branch to the neglect of more important studies. It is true a knowledge of arithmetic is indispensable in all ordinary operations of life, but the knowledge necessary for the practical work of life is soon and easily acquired, and all beyond this is of comparatively slight importance compared with many other branches.

Mental or oral and written arithmetic should be taught together. There is no need of two text-books on arithmetic in common schools. All the principles and examples necessary to illustrate them might be comprised in one handy volume, which could be used alike by the primary and advanced pupils in our country schools.

The first thing a child learns about arithmetic is to count. This he will learn to some extent with little or no instruction. Exercises in counting, and practice in forming the nine digits may be given in connection with reading. (See p. 75.)

The teacher, in organizing a country school, will find it necessary to start a class in the first principles of arithmetic. He should begin with addition, it being supposed the pupils are able to count to one hundred. Objects should be used at first, such as pieces of chalk, sticks, grains of corn, beans, books, marks on the black-board, balls on a frame, or the fingers. Commence with easy examples and advance gradually to more difficult sums. Objects should be discarded as soon as the pupil acquires the idea of addition and can add with some degree of readiness. Examples consisting of single columns of figures may be placed on the board and the pupils required to add them on their slates as a preparation for the lesson. These examples should consist at first of but two or three numbers, using the smaller digits and advancing to more numbers and larger digits until the pupil is able to add a column of a dozen or more figures, using all the digits from one to nine. In this way they will soon learn the addition table by using it. Oral and written exercises should be given in about equal proportions. Pupils will soon learn by observation to write numbers above nine so that they can write the answers to the examples given if they do not go above hundreds. The next step is to teach the first principles of notation and numeration. Show that the value of a digit depends upon the place it occupies. Explain the use of the cipher and teach the places up to thousands. Drill until the pupils can name the first four places in any order you may point to them. Exercise the class in writing numbers from one to thousands. Next you may teach the process of carrying, and drill in adding more than one column of figures until they are able to add any sum the numbers of which are less than thousands. Subtraction should be next taught, using objects at first until they get the idea, then exercises in subtracting in one column and then in two or more columns where the upper digit is always the largest, then the process of borrowing. Examples should be given until they are able to subtract thousands. Promiscuous examples in addition and subtraction may now be given and the method of proving subtraction explained.

Further instruction and exercises in notation and numeration may next be given. Make haste slowly. There is no end to the examples you may give your class as practice in what you have already given them instruction. If you have not books containing examples, write them on the board where they can be seen by the whole class. They need the exercises for practice, and the employment, they give, will keep them out of mischief.

The next step will be to learn the multiplication table. It is best learned by using it. The teacher will, of course, preface the study of the table by an explanation of the principle of multiplication. He may illustrate by objects or by making marks on the board showing that it is a short method of addition where the numbers to be added are alike. Examples should be given where the multiplier and multiplicand are single digits, and next where the multiplicand is a large number, explaining the process of carrying as in addition, and next where both factors consist of several digits. Practice multiplying numbers until the table is learned, giving occasional review exercises in addition and subtraction. Oral drills on the tables should be given daily. Before advancing further see that the pupils can add, subtract and multiply with facility.

Division is next in order, and with some pupils it will take a great deal of practice to make them perfect. Drill as in the other rules, and for variety review what has been taught. Give examples combining the four fundamental rules, and keep up oral exercises and drills in notation and numeration. Teach the use of the signs $+$, $-$, $\times$, $\div$, $=$. Addition, subtraction, multiplication, division, and notation and numeration are called the fundamental rules, because all operations of arithmetic are carried on by means of them. The teacher should see that his pupils are thoroughly drilled in them before advancing further. Our text-books do not give a sufficient number of examples. Do not tire the pupils by requiring them to work the same examples over again, but give them new ones illustrating the same principles. This observation will hold good all the way through the book. I have seen pupils who had "worked," as they said, half way through the text-book, yet could not write nor read large numbers nor solve examples in long division.

I can see no propriety in putting puzzling examples embracing the fundamental rules immediately after division, as is the case in Ray's arithmetic. Such problems are rarely ever solved by the pupils without the aid of the teacher. Examples should be given embracing these rules, but they should be plain and simple, intended to give exercise in the processes of adding, subtracting, multiplying and dividing, and not to test the child's skill in reasoning. He is not yet prepared to reason to such an extent. Of what use can an example like the following be to a child who has just learned the four arithmetical processes?

A cistern of 360 gals. has 2 pipes, one will fill it in 15 hours, the other empty it in 20 hours. If both pipes are left open, how many hours will the cistern be in filling?—*Ray's Arith., Part 3d, p.* 64.

An exactly similar example is given under Analysis on p. 265 of the same book. The teacher must use his own judgment about such matters and not blindly follow the text-book. He can give examples of his own which the pupils can solve, and which will give exercise in the processes they have learned, and such examples as the above should be omitted until the pupil has acquired the skill to solve them himself.

Processes should be taught before rules, or rather the rules developed from the processes. The inductive method is the best in teaching arithmetic. Thus far the pupil has only learned processes, but they are processes he must use all through life, and are of more importance practically than the more abstract principles underlying them. When the pupil has reached a more mature age and greater intellectual development, the more abstract parts may be taken up.

Examples somewhat like the following may be given as exercises in the fundamental rules:

Write 495. Annex a cipher. This multiplies it by 10. From this product let 495 be subtracted as many times as possible. The operation will appear thus:

4950
495
―――
4455
495
―――
3960
495
―――
3465
495
―――
2970
495
―――
2475
495
―――
1980
495
―――
1485
495
―――
990
495
―――
495
495
―――
000

It will be seen that after ten subtractions the remainder is naught. This proves that division is but "a short method of making many subtractions of the same number." Any other number than ten may be used as the multiplier, and it will be found that to make the final remainder naught there must be as many subtractions as there are units in the multiplier.

The operation may be reversed; by starting with naught and adding 495 ten times successively the number 4950 will be reached, proving that multiplication is a short method of adding equal numbers.

By giving such examples as the above much exercise can be given the pupil with little work on the part of the teacher. The pupils make their own examples. Exercise in proving subtraction, multiplication and division should be given, and some of the more important contractions taught.

Having had sufficient drill in handling simple integral numbers in their fundamental relations, the pupil is now ready to commence with

COMPOUND OR DENOMINATE NUMBERS.

United States Money, though really a form of decimals, is placed under this head by some authors, and as it is simple and affords much exercise in the fundamental rules, and involving only one new idea, that of the separatrix, it is best taken up here. Particular attention should be paid to the fact that the separatrix is used to separate dollars and cents; that it is always placed after dollars and before cents, and should never in any case be omitted. Pupils need frequent reminding of this fact, and the teacher should see that the habit of attention to this matter is formed while very young. Explain to them that if this little matter is not attended to, serious trouble will arise in after operations of arithmetic. I have seen pupils working almost through the book who would make blunders of this kind constantly, and get examples so confused that they could not tell what they were doing, and all because they had never been taught the importance of the separatrix. Explain that in U. S. money ten units of one denomination make one of the next higher, and consequently they can be handled the same as simple numbers, the only difference being that dollars and cents are always to be separated by the point. The fact that cents always occupy two places should also be impressed upon their minds, explaining that accounts are kept in dollars, cents and mills, and that dimes and cents are counted together as cents, and therefore when the number of cents is less than ten there are no dimes, and a cipher must be placed next to the separatrix in the place of dimes. You may tell them that a mill is the tenth part of a cent or the one thousandth part of a dollar, and is not coined, being too small, but is of importance in calculating large amounts. They will understand this better when they have studied decimals.

Give numerous examples in adding, subtracting, multiplying and dividing U. S. money, many more than are given in the text-books. Examples of merchants' bills are given in most books, but the teacher should add many more, as they are of great practical value. In giving the example of a merchant's bill, use the name of some merchant in the neighborhood whom the pupils know, and give always the current price of items. Pay particular attention to the neatness of a bill, using abbreviations, capital letters and punctuation properly. Require pupils to copy the examples from the board as written by the teacher. An example of this kind will appear something like the following:

IN COUNTRY SCHOOLS. 107

BUSSEY, IOWA, July 16, 1879.
JAS. H. SIMMS.
BOUGHT OF THEO. WEST:

11 lbs. Coffee	@ $	.25...............................
17 lbs. Sugar	"	.08...............................
2 Boxes Matches	"	.10...............................
3 Pair Shoes	"	2.40...............................
12 Yds. Prints	"	.07...............................
23 Yds. Muslin	"	.12...............................
3 Spools Thread	"	.05...............................
2 Doz. Buttons	"	.03...............................

Rec'd Payment. $

THEO. WEST.

The more apt pupils may be requested to make out and write on their slates bills of their own. This will, however, be a good exercise for review after the pupil has passed through Compound Numbers.

Reduction of Compound Numbers may now be taught. The tables should be learned by using them. If numerous examples are given and sufficient drill be had at recitation upon each table, the tables will soon be learned without the necessity of telling pupils they must commit them to memory. See that examples are written neatly and all denominations expressed by their proper abbreviations, attention being paid to pronunciation. Illustrate by familiar objects, the different weights and measures in common use. (See p. 39.) Do not neglect the oral drill on each table. Give practical examples, such as involve dimensions of the school-room, tables, desks, school-yard, fences, etc.

It is a good exercise to require pupils to copy the tables from the books on their slates. Cloth Measure and Ale and Beer Measure not being now in use, should be omitted if found in the text-book, and Circular Measure and English Money deferred until the pupil has made greater advancement. Review by numerous promiscuous examples for practice, giving frequent drills on the tables.

Addition, Subtraction, Multiplication and Division of Compound Numbers may come next. Explain that numbers of the same denomination only, can be added or subtracted. Show that in simple numbers ten units of one denomination make one of the next higher, but in Compound Numbers some other number than ten is used. Explain the process of carrying and borrowing. Give practical examples in subtraction; let the pupil find difference between dates, and require each one to find his own exact age in this way. Longitude and Time should be omitted until the pupil is more advanced.

Review Compound Numbers until pupils understand what you have attempted to teach them. Do not turn the class back in the book. This is always discouraging. But give a number of review lessons, taking up those parts in which you find the class to be the most deficient. This rule will hold good always. Never turn a pupil back, but advance slowly, giving plenty of exercises, and review frequently until all is thoroughly understood.

The pupil is now ready to investigate some of the properties of numbers, generally considered under the head of factoring.

A great deal of preliminary drill is here necessary to get pupils to comprehend the definitions. It is nonsense to require them to commit to memory definitions and rules the meaning of which they can not comprehend. Pupils always expect their lessons in arithmetic to be mostly examples, and they will take little interest in studying definitions. Give numerous examples first and develop the definitions from them. Impress on their minds the idea of a factor, a multiple and a prime number. Teach the process of finding the least common multiple and greatest common divisor, leaving the demonstrations until a future period, explaining that though they may see no importance in these processes at present they will as they advance in the book.

The process of cancellation may next be taught, after which the pupil may commence *Fractions*.

The idea of a fraction should be illustrated by taking some object, as an apple, a stick or a piece of paper and dividing it into equal parts. Then show how a fraction is written, and explain the terms numerator (numberer) and denominator (namer). Numerous examples should be given in writing and reading fractions, and thorough drill, until the class has the idea of a fraction and understands the terms, numerator and denominator.

The process of reduction may follow, remembering to make haste slowly, giving numerous examples and frequent reviews. I need not discourse further on this subject. The teacher, who has carried a class successfully thus far, will readily see what is needed to make proficient scholars in fractions.

Fractional Compound Numbers may next be studied. Examples in U. S. money and merchants' bills involving fractions should be given. Decimal Fractions may follow. Review simple numbers, showing how they increase and decrease in a tenfold ratio. Impress the importance of the decimal point. Compare U. S. money with decimals, showing the advantages of the decimal system.

Percentage should be studied before Ratio and Proportion. Impress particularly the fact that *per cent.* means so many hundredths, without regard to dollars and cents. I have made it a particular matter of notice, and have observed that more than half the pupils I have had under my care who have gone through the book had the idea that per cent. had reference particularly to dollars and cents. This may seem strange to a good teacher, but it is a fact. I may have happened to have followed poor teachers, which would account for it. Many examples such as the following should be given :

A man had 64 hogs. 25 per cent. of them died. How many were left?

In studying Interest, pupils should have exercise in writing promissory notes and computing the interest on them.

Explain Insurance, Stocks, Brokerage, Commission, Discount, Present Worth, Taxes, Customs and Duties, Bonds, Coupons, etc., by familiar illustrations, and make them plainer than text-books usually do.

Such subjects as Alligation, Exchange, Duodecimals, Arithmetical and Geometrical Progression should be omitted until the pupil has had thorough drill on the more important parts of arithmetic.

The subject of Mensuration being of practical value to all classes should receive considerable attention. Let the pupil measure the school-room and find its capacity in cubic feet, bushels, gallons, etc. Measuring fields, corn-cribs, granaries, wagon-boxes, timber, etc., is of practical value to farmers' boys, and such the country teacher has mainly under his care.

The irregularity of attendance in country schools is so great that it is a difficult matter to conduct a class in arithmetic properly. The pupil is out of school a week and the class has gone so far ahead that he can no longer keep up with it. Must the class be held back to accommodate such pupils? Certainly not. The teacher must have a number of classes, so that those who are too dull, or too irregular in attendance, may fall back and join a lower class. If he has not time to give a regular recitation each day to every class, he can give them a drill on alternate days and examples for practice on intervening days. In this way he can manage to reach all. He should, however, take notice of each pupil every day in some manner. He may do this by assigning one class examples to work on the black-board while he is conducting the recitation for the other class. He can then devote a few minutes to inspecting the work on the board. Each pupil should be allowed to travel as fast as he can, provided he thoroughly understands what he passes over. An apt pupil should never be held back to keep pace with a dull one.

GENERAL OBSERVATIONS.

I would call attention to the following points, most of which are a recapitulation of this chapter:

1. As a rule, teach easiest parts first.

2. Do not hurry through the book, but give plenty of exercises under each subject.

3. Teach processes first, principles next. Teach the rules by stating the steps in the process.

4. Never require rules, definitions or tables to be committed to memory, but let them be learned by use.

5. Let the pupil learn the explanations of rules from the book, the teacher only pointing them out and explaining the language of the book.

6. Pay particular attention to the most practical parts of arithmetic, such as pupils will most likely use in after life.

7. Give preliminary drill on each new subject.

8. Require pupils to always use shortest methods of obtaining a result, but insist on clearness of expression and neatness of work.

9. An oral analysis of problems, involving only numbers small enough to be held in the memory, should always precede a written process. The first step then would be the oral drill in analysis; second, the written process, and third the rule, which is simply the statement of the several steps of the process. For example, the teacher should show analytically that $\frac{3}{4}$ of $\frac{2}{5}$ is $\frac{3}{10}$, and then deduce the written process for finding a fraction of a fraction, or that 4 is 25 per cent. of 16, and from that the process of finding what per cent. one number is of another, or that $\frac{2}{3} \div \frac{1}{2}$ is $1\frac{1}{3}$, and deduce the process of division of fractions and explain the reason for inverting the divisor. There may be some exceptions to this with young pupils, as for example, in finding the greatest common divisor and least common multiple.

10. Review often.

CHAPTER IV.

GEOGRAPHY.

"Geography can not be taught in any proper sense of the word by maps or a bald and wearisome nomenclature of countries, cities, mountains and rivers. What is wanted is that these should be intimately blended with the history of the world, of nature and the history of mankind, thereby better fixing the whole in the memory and giving to Geography its true rank among the sciences. The change thus indicated is in progress, but much is still wanted for its full accomplishment." *Sir Henry Holland.*

Geography as taught in many schools—merely by question and answer, with an occasional map drill—is of little practical value, but in the hands of a competent instructor who *teaches*, rather than hears a class recite, it is an interesting and valuable study.

It has been my experience that but a small proportion of the pupils of a country school who are of the proper age study Geography. Upon inquiry the universal reason given was that they did not like the study. Now, whose fault is this? Certainly the teacher's. The teacher should awaken an interest in this study in his school, and the way to do this is to teach it properly and persuade pupils to enter the class. If he teaches it as he should and succeeds in getting a pupil to enter the class and remain one week, I will venture to assert that that pupil will remain for the whole term. In my opinion there is no study of greater importance. It is a branch of knowledge which a Humboldt, a Ritter and a Guyot have adorned, and deserves no mean place among the knowledges of the earth.

There need be but two classes in Geography in a country school, a primary and an advanced.

With a beginning class I would proceed somewhat as follows: I am supposing the class is composed of pupils who have never studied the subject. I would begin with an oral drill on direction, next develop the idea of a map by drawing a map of the school room. I would draw the boundary lines on the board, explaining that the top of the diagram will represent north, the bottom south, etc., and ask the pupils to step to the board and make a mark to represent the location of the stove, the teacher's desk, etc., and proceed until the pupils themselves have mapped out the school-room and located all the principal objects in it. The next step would be to map the school-yard, locating the school-house, the outhouses, trees and other objects. I might proceed from this to the surrounding farms; but perhaps enough has been shown to develop the idea of a map, that it is a representation of a part or the whole of the earth's surface. Next, I may ask some questions about what is found on the surface of the earth. By a few leading questions I will obtain from the class the facts that rivers, lakes, mountains, cities, towns, etc., are to be seen on the earth's surface. Then I will tell them that we are going to learn all about what we would find on the surface of the earth if we would travel over it, and about the different kinds of people and what they are doing, and many things that are very interesting and useful; that men have learned these things by traveling and observing and have written them in books for us to study that we may learn without traveling far from home. With this preliminary drill they are ready to take up a primary work on Geography and begin with the study of the form of the earth, the divisions of land and water, etc. If possible, use a globe to illustrate, if not, get a substitute for one, an apple or a ball. Explain some of the more obvious modes of proving the rotundity of the earth. If possible take the class to a lake shore or river bank and show them capes, bays, islands, etc. Such objects can generally be found on a small scale along a river or lake shore.

The topic method of teaching Geography can be made successful even with beginners, but the topics must be modified to suit their capacities.

Most text-books on Geography are filled with questions, and the teacher is tempted to fall into a rote manner of teaching and content himself with asking the questions and hearing the pupils answer. While I would not ignore questions in teaching, I would certainly try to avoid depending on them.

Slates should be used by primary classes in preparing their lessons. The names of all the prominent objects of study in the lesson should be carefully written on the slate. For example, let the pupil write the words continent, island, cape, river, lake, etc., on the slate and be required to find the definition of the terms in the book. The teacher may write on the board the principal points of the lesson for the pupil to copy. In studying a map the teacher should require the pupils to write a certain number of cities, rivers, mountains, etc., allowing the pupil to select what he thinks the most important. Let the pupil write also a certain number of the products of a country, as wheat, corn, coal, iron, gold, silver, etc. Lessons may be assigned as they are laid off in the book, but a written exercise should always accompany them. Frequent review lessons should be given, involving all points of importance the pupil has passed over.

Map drills should be had daily, sometimes the teacher pointing to the map and the pupils answering as called upon or occasionally in concert, and sometimes the pupils in turn point out places on the map as mentioned by the teacher.

It is a good exercise to take an ideal trip, as, for example, starting with Chicago, the teacher and class sail in imagination to New York, mentioning and commenting upon all the prominent places of interest they would pass on the route. I will here mention a few such routes: From London to St. Petersburg *via* Gibralter, following the coasts of Spain, Italy and Greece, and through Constantinople and Black sea, and up the river and overland across Russia. From St. Petersburg, through the Baltic and along coasts of Denmark, Holland and Belgium, to London. From London, again, to Pekin, around Cape of Good Hope and *via* Calcutta. From New York to New Orleans, following coast, and from thence to Pittsburg *via* Cin-

cinnati and by railroad back again to New York. A whaling voyage from Boston to the Arctic ocean. A trip from Philadelphia to Rio Janeiro for coffee. Such exercises may be made extremely interesting to children and are excellent for review. Mention may be made of the governments, races, productions, curiosities and other peculiarities of countries as they are passed on these imaginary voyages.

Do not attempt to teach too many things, but by frequent reviews fix thoroughly the most important points. For example, if a pupil learns that a certain State produces three or four certain staples, and can tell whether it is level or mountainous, can mention the capital and largest city and locate them, the principal river and lake, if any, and can give its boundaries and comparative size and tell what direction from his own State—if these points are fixed by thorough drill he will remember them longer and the knowledge be of more practical benefit than if he had learned every little river, lake, town and all the minutia of detail, only to be forgotten perhaps before the next recitation. (See page 39.)

It is a good idea to go over the main points of each lesson in concert as a kind of recapitulation at the close of each recitation.

Suggestive questions, such as the following, may sometimes be put to primary classes:

What city is world-renowned for carpets? In what city would you ride in a gondola instead of an omnibus? In what country do the women always go out veiled and the men wear loose, flowing robes and sit cross-legged and smoke opium? What island is celebrated for its peat bogs, potatoes, oats and flax? etc., etc.

Review lessons may be given somewhat as follows: Each pupil is assigned a subject for investigation and report, something easy, yet which will require a search of the book, as, for example, John is told to find all the countries in which mention is made of gold, Mary of silver, Henry of lions, Willie of elephants, Carrie of diamonds, etc. The names of the countries when found may be written on the slates, which are brought to the recitation and laid upon the teacher's desk. The teacher takes up a slate and calls on the owner of it to mention from memory as much as he can of what he has written. The others may criticise errors and add to it if they can.

For primary classes it is best that all the pupils have the same text-book, but an advanced class may be taught entirely by the topic method, and it is even better if each member of the class has a different author. I have used a topic list something like the following:

1. Position, { Boundaries, Latitude and Longitude.
2. Size.
3. Mountains and surface generally.
4. Rivers and lakes.
5. Coast line, { Gulfs, bays, straits, etc. Capes, islands, etc.
6. Climate.
7. Productions, { Animal, Vegetable, Mineral.

8. Occupations,
  { Agricultural and grazing,
   Commerce and fisheries,
   Mining,
   Manufacturing.
9. Government, education and religion.
10. Capital and largest city.
11. Other cities and places of interest.
12. History.
13. Population.
14. Miscellaneous.

This is to be used in studying the text of the several countries. It should be written on the blackboard and copied by the pupils and pasted in their books. The teacher will explain the outline where necessary. In giving latitude and longitude, countries should be compared with each other, foreign countries with our own States, and the States with each other. The absolute size of a few countries should be remembered, especially the pupil's own State, and other States and countries compared with it. Very large and very small States and countries should be compared, as Rhode Island and Texas, England and Russia, etc. In studying surface I have given mountains as the most prominent objects, but the pupil should be led to mention height above sea level, plateaus, volcanoes, basins, water-sheds, etc. The absolute height of the most important peaks in each country should be remembered and the direction of the mountain chains noted. Rivers should be described by telling where they rise, what course they pursue and into what they empty. Lakes, either salt or fresh, having outlets or inlets, both or neither, depth, height above sea level, etc. The pupil should be taught that climate depends on latitude, proximity to or remoteness from large bodies of water, character and proximity of ocean currents, height of land, slope, character of soil, prevailing winds, etc.

Under head of animal productions, the wild and domestic animals should be mentioned, and the articles produced from them, as furs, wool, feathers, leather, tallow, honey, beeswax, glue, bone-dust, bone, horn, silk, etc. The vegetable productions are such as grain, mentioning the different kinds, fruits, flax, potatoes, gums, resins, medicines, dye-stuffs, timber, turpentine, tar, etc. The mineral productions are the metals, building material, as marble, granite, limestone, sand, lime, potter's clay, mineral paints, precious stones, etc. Under the head of commerce might be mentioned the principal articles of export and import. Under manufacturing, the different articles manufactured. Under head of history, if one of the States of the Union, its first settlement, when, where and by whom, date of admission, etc.; if other countries, some of the principal points in their history, as great battles, changes of government, etc. Under head of miscellaneous, mention may be made of anything that would be of interest and which can not well be brought under any of the previous heads, such as natural curiosities, races, languages and dialects spoken, peculiar customs of the people, national character, etc.

The above list is flexible enough to adapt itself to an advanced class in any school. There is, of course, great difference in pupils, and the teacher must recognize this in teaching any branch and adapt his plans to them. The pupil is to be made understand that he is expected to obtain the information here outlined, and it need not matter where he obtains it, whether from this author or from that, or partly from one and partly from another. He may learn from travelers, from miscellaneous works or from newspapers, from any source, provided he gets the information in such a way that he can tell it. Dull and backward pupils will need to be questioned to bring out their knowledge, but this should not be done where it can be avoided. The pupil should be taught to rely upon himself and tell what he knows without being questioned. Pupils who have been taught in the old rote manner may make objections to this manner of study, but the true teacher will soon win them to his own views. He should explain to them the advantages, and at first modify the plan so as not to make too sudden a change.

This topic list can not be used in all classes. Special outlines should be given in studying some of the points of Mathematical and Physical Geography. Review lessons may be given by special outlines; for example, lakes may be given as a lesson and outlined on the board somewhat as follows:

Lakes.
    1. Origin.
    2. Classes.
        1. As to character of water.
        2. As to outlets and inlets.
    3. Elevation.
    4. Uses.
    5. Principal lakes of the world.
        1. As to commercial importance.
        2. As to elevation.
        3. As to size.
        4. As to beautiful scenery.
        5. As to any other peculiarity.

Mountains, volcanoes, seas, gulfs and bays, oceans, rivers, etc., may be outlined in a similar manner. Such special outlines for review are of great practical value, gathering up, as it were, the knowledge which has been attained into parcels and labeling them.

A special outline should also be given for the pupil's own State. This should be very full and minute, embracing all the points which would be worth remembering. Swinton's Geography develops this plan of paying particular attention to home and local Geography and gives such an outline for the study of any particular State. The teacher, however, who is acquainted with his own State and has paid some attention to outlining can easily produce one which will suit his purpose better than could be given here.

The teacher should have a map of the State showing counties and townships, and if possible a map of the county. These maps should be provided by school boards for every school-house. The teacher may, however, do as I have done in several instances, draw on the wall with colored chalk a map of the county, showing townships, and in the township the school-house was in showing school district, school houses, roads, streams, etc. I copied them from borrowed maps. (See p. 187.)

Some system of map drawing should be pursued, but I would caution the teacher against making a hobby of it. It is a means and not an end. The teacher should recognize also the different capacities of his pupils in this respect. Some will seem to have a natural ability to draw, while with others it is a difficult matter to interest them or teach them to draw even passably. Particular pains should be taken in drawing the pupil's own State, but if it is one difficult to draw do not give it as the first lesson. Practice them in drawing some State of regular and easy outline. I need not say anything further on this head, as all text-books now give instructions in map drawing.

For advanced pupils the teacher should prepare questions which will lead them to think and apply their knowledge, questions which can not be answered in the language of any book, but such as the pupil must deduce the answer from his own knowledge of the facts. As an example of such questions the teacher will ask why New England is a manufacturing country; why Iowa and Illinois raise so many hogs; why gold and silver are not found in Illinois; why sheep are raised more extensively in Ohio and California; why New Jersey and Delaware raise so many fruits and vegetables; why Iowa, Kansas and Nebraska have so few large cities; why education is not more universally diffused throughout the Southern States; why Indian corn is not raised in England; why England has such fine breeds of cattle and horses; what would be the effect on the climate of Italy, France, Greece and Spain if the Desert of Sahara were turned into a sea; why the peculiar dry climate of Colorado; why so many Spanish names of towns, etc., in the Territories and States west of the Mississippi; why so many French names along the St. Lawrence and Mississippi; why Quito, being on the equator, has such a pleasant climate, etc. The teacher, who is well versed in a knowledge of Geography, as he should be, can multiply such questions to any necessary extent. A few such questions should be assigned at one time, and the pupils allowed two or three days to prepare their answers.

In the hands of a live teacher a class in Geography may be made the most enthusiastic and interesting class of the school. There are some points in teaching Geography which may be called Geographical Recreations. For example, the origin and significance of names of places and countries. If the teacher will consult Webster's Unabridged he will find material of this kind. Also, the popular names of cities and States, as Garden City, Crescent City, Hoosier State, Hawkeye State, etc. (See p. —.)

The formation of some of the physical features of the earth's surface may be illustrated in a simple and pleasing manner by means of a large tray made of boards, in the shape of a box, about three inches deep and two feet wide by three or four feet in length. A dry goods box will answer by cutting it down to the required depth. Fill this with wet sand to within half an inch of the top. Mountains, hills, plateaus and plains may be formed with the sand. A volcano may be made by placing a piece of unslacked lime in a mountain and wetting the sand. In a little while the lime will slack and the sides of the mountain will become hot and crack open and an opening appear in the top, from which will issue steam and powdered lime. By inclining the tray and pouring a shower of water from a sprinkling can, the formation of rivers may be shown. If the sand is so arranged that the lowest part be along the center the water will collect and form a large river and its tributaries. The washing down of the mountains to form plains is also illustrated. The formation of cañons may be illustrated by taking clay and mixing it with water until a mud is formed, which, when allowed to dry in the sun or by the fire, will crack open, making large fissures, and by pouring water the fissures will be enlarged, showing how, in the course of ages, the internal heat of the earth and the erosive action of water have dug these wonderful ditches.

The latitude of a few prominent places should be fixed in the mind. The following is a good exercise for this purpose: The teacher, taking a globe or map of the world, and selecting a certain parallel, say 40°, says, "I find on or near this parallel Columbus, O., Philadelphia, Pa., Rome, Italy," etc. Then, selecting another, say 30°, he says, "I find on this New Orleans, La., St. Augustine, Fla., etc. What is the latitude of Philadelphia, of New Orleans, of Rome?" etc. Then, selecting another parallel, he adds a few more places and asks questions promiscuously as before, the pupils answering in concert. In this way a short drill occasionally will fix the latitude of the most prominent places in the world in the pupil's memory. Other places may be compared with them. For example, if one wishes to know the latitude of Mobile, Ala., he has only to remember that it is a little further north than New Orleans, and therefore near 30°. About ten years ago I participated in a drill of this kind at a teachers' institute in which T. W. Harvey was instructor, and I do not think I shall ever forget the latitude of a number of places I there learned in a few minutes' drill. The teacher who is alive to his work will find many such expedients as I have here given, and will need no further suggestions from me in regard to teaching Geography.

CHAPTER V.

GRAMMAR.

J. R. Sypher, in "The Art of Teaching School," says: "If, in the spelling classes, the uses of capital letters and punctuation marks have been noted—as should be the case in spelling from dictation and discourse—and if, in the reading classes, the structure of sentences, the meaning of words and the uses of punctuation marks have been properly studied, there is little remaining to be taught on the subject of Grammar, to pupils in the public schools, that properly comes within the scope of these institutions." There is much truth in this. I have advocated particular attention to defining, punctuation, use of capitals, etc., in reading and spelling classes, because these points are essential to the practical every-day duties of life, and from the fact that comparatively few pupils who attend our country schools ever take up the study of Grammar.

The country teacher is expected to have a class in Grammar, and it should be taught in our country schools, but I protest against the manner in which it is usually taught. There is no need of, nor no time for, a primary text-book in Grammar in a country school, and indeed in any other school. The primary instruction in Grammar should be given in reading and spelling classes, and by general criticisms and oral drills in connection with every other subject. That is, the pupil should be taught to use the English language properly. All written and oral exercises where the pupil is required to use language are exercises in Grammar. The teacher should always use accurate language, and correct every error made by the pupils. This should be carried to the play-ground, and everywhere the pupil comes in contact with the teacher, provided it can be done without giving offense to any one. Primary Grammar should consist of language lessons, and every lesson, on whatever subject, should be also a language lesson. I am using the word "Grammar" in the sense understood from the definitions given by nearly, if not all, writers of text-books on the subject, and from the definition of the term given by Webster—that is, that it is the science which teaches us how to use language correctly. Wickersham, in "Methods of Instruction," page 246, says: "Grammar is the science of sentences. * * * Grammar is not an art. Composition treats of the art of speaking and writing." Hon. E. E. White, in "The National Teacher," says: "Notwithstanding Lindley Murray's definition, Grammar is not the means for acquiring the art of speaking and writing correctly. It is at best only the finishing instrument. The correct use of language must be learned, as every other art is learned, *by practice under intelligent guidance.* School training should furnish this practice in a large measure. There can not well be too much of it. It should enter into every recitation, and besides have a separate place in the daily programme. Composition should be taught as faithfully as arithmetic."

I give these extracts for what they are worth. They simply show the difficulty of defining terms. I will add that it is the duty of teachers to teach that which will cause pupils to think, and at the same time to express their thoughts, either with the tongue or pen, in the most fluent, elegant and correct manner. They can be led to improve their thinking powers to a greater or less degree by the study of any subject whatever; and the power of expressing thought is taught under the heads of Reading, Spelling, Defining, Grammar, Rhetoric, Composition, Elocution, Oratory, etc. I will refer the reader to the definitions of these terms given by Webster and by the various authors of text-books on the respective subjects.

The question, with the country teacher having a class before him with text-books in Grammar in their hands, is, what part of the book shall be taught. I will answer in a general way by saying, teach that which will aid them most in expressing thought, either by tongue or pen. But, to be more specific, I will suppose a class who have never studied the subject technically to have in their hands Harvey's, or Holbrook's, or Clark's, or Adams', or any other suitable text-book for common schools, and I will tell you where I think you ought to begin.

The first lesson in technical Grammar should be on the structure of simple sentences.

Write a word, as *run*, on the blackboard. Ask the

class to tell you the name of something that runs. They will probably say: "Horses run," "A dog runs," "Water runs," etc. You may tell them that it is not correct, and they can see that it would not sound well to say "Horses runs," or "A dog run." Next you may write the sentence, *Horses run*, on the board, and tell them that it is a thought expressed in words and is called a sentence. Then give an exercise in producing sentences. Have the class give half a dozen sentences similar to this, and you may write them on the board. Next you may teach them the principal parts of a sentence, the subject and predicate. Be sure that pupils have a clear idea of these terms. I remember that when a boy studying Grammar the definitions of subject and predicate were for a long time not understood. I did not know what was meant by *affirmed*, when the book and teacher said, "The subject is that of which something is affirmed." It sounded big and frightful, and I never had a clear idea until I saw somewhere the definition, "The subject is that of which something is said or written." Now, I might have been an unusually dull boy—in some respects I know I was—but are there not dull boys in every class? The best teacher makes a subject plain to the dullest in his class. Give plenty of oral exercises, somewhat as follows: Chalk is brittle. What is brittle? What is said about chalk? What is the subject of this sentence? Why? What is the predicate? Why? Require class to write three or four sentences for each lesson. Write a word, as "*Fire*," on the board. Ask the class to write as many predicates as they can to this subject; also write a predicate, and require them to write a number of subjects. Most text-books now give model exercises which will suggest the oral drill to the teacher.

After several lessons on the simple sentence, and when the pupils thoroughly understand the principal parts of a sentence, I would study the noun. The first lesson would be an outline of the noun, to be made out by teacher and pupils. The teacher writes the main heads and tells where to write the subordinate parts. The outline, when completed, will stand as follows, the parts in italics showing what was written by the teacher and those in Roman the parts filled in by the pupils:

Noun.

   Classes.

      General.

         Common.
         Proper.

      Special.

         Abstract.
         Verbal.
         Collective.
         Class.

   Properties.

      Gender.

         Masculine.
         Feminine.
         Common.
         Neuter.

Person.
　First.
　Second.
　Third.

Number.
　Singular.
　Plural.

Case.
　Nominative.
　Possessive.
　Objective.
　Absolute.

Pupils who have had exercise in outlining in other studies, perhaps would be able to produce the above without the aid of the teacher. But this is intended to be merely suggestive, and the teacher must proceed according to the circumstances present. Several lessons may be made from this outline, discussing all the parts until a pretty thorough knowledge of the noun is secured, so far as can be, without reference to other parts of speech. The parsing of nouns, so far as the pupil is able from what he has learned, and exercises in writing sentences containing nouns, illustrating their properties and classes, should be a part of every lesson. The advantage of writing parsing lessons will be obvious to any thinking teacher. It will secure exercise in spelling, punctuation, capitalization and penmanship, will be more interesting, and lead to definite and accurate thinking. The teachers should have some particular order of parsing, and require all pupils to follow it. In another place will be given models for the written parsing of each part of speech.

In a similar manner to the noun the verb may be studied. An outline giving classes and properties is to be made out and the different parts of it discussed. The more difficult parts may be omitted until a future time, taking only such as are usually given in large print in text-books. This outline is to be studied the same as the outline of the noun, taking a small portion at each lesson, and giving oral and written exercises as before.

The next step is to introduce the objective element into the sentence. The pupil now will understand that a sentence must have a subject and a predicate, and may have an object. The pronoun may be studied next, to be followed by the adjective, adverb, preposition, conjunction and interjection, each to be outlined and discussed as above. After a discussion of the adjective, adverbial and independent elements of a sentence, a review of the parts of speech, beginning again with the noun, should be had, studying them in their relations to each other. This time the pupils can make the outlines themselves, adding all the minor points. Compound and complex sentences may next be considered, and the lessons varied with plenty of written exercises in parsing, writing sentences and diagramming.

The teacher is now ready to introduce the subject of composition writing. This is a great bugbear to most pupils in country schools, but it is the fault of no one but the teacher. I remember, when a boy, attending a term of school taught by a lady who required, every Friday, a composition from each pupil who was old enough to write. By dint of coaxing and threatening she succeeded in getting every one to try but me. I was obstinate, and no coaxing or threatening would induce me to attempt what I was confident I could not do. The pupils wrote compositions on such subjects as Spring, Autumn, sunset, education, and their thoughts and language were almost sublime. It is said there is but one step from the sublime to the ridiculous. They had almost taken that step backward. Years afterward I attended a select school, and the teacher was a true teacher, and instead of *requiring* us to write compositions he taught us *how* to write them, and then it was only necessary to give us the privilege.

Sentence writing is the first step to composition writing, and if the teacher has thus far given sufficient exercise in that branch the next step will be easy enough. All that is necessary for a composition is to put together a number of sentences relating to the same subject. But no one can write sentences or composition unless he has something to write about. A single word is not sufficient for a subject for a beginner. He must have an outline or skeleton of what he is going to write about. This the teacher must provide, and he must give instruction on points of the outline, at first, until the pupil has acquired sufficient skill and command of language and power of thought to construct the outline for himself.

Beginners, if left to themselves, will generally choose some broad theme, as Education, Intemperance, etc., not knowing that it is far easier to write on a more restricted subject. Men of such broad and liberal culture as Herbert Spencer may take such a subject as Education for an essay. The brilliant essayists of this country, as Whipple, Lowell and Holland, may take for their themes Humanity, Liberty, Truth, etc., but a beginner should choose something more concrete and restricted, such as Wheat, Apples, Dogs, Cats, A Walk in the Country, What I Saw at the Fair, etc.

The simplest form of essay writing, perhaps, is to write a number of questions and require the pupil to write out the answers in full and connect them together. For example, let me suppose the subject to be "My Dog." The teacher will write a series of questions, as follows: Have you a dog? What kind of a dog is he? What is his color? Has he long hair? What kind of a tail has he? Will he bark at strangers? Is he cross? Will he do what you tell him? Will you name some of the smart things he can do? Does he dislike children? What is his name?

The essay, when written, will appear something like the following:

MY DOG.

I have a large Newfoundland dog. He is all over black, except a white ring around his neck. He has long, shaggy hair, and his tail is long and bushy and curls up over his back. He will bark at strangers, but he is not cross, and will not bite any one unless he thinks they are going to steal something. He will do almost anything I tell him. He will bring the cows and horses up from the meadow, will fetch sticks out of the water, and carry a basket in his mouth. He is not cross to children, but will let them ride on his back or pull him round, and seems to enjoy the fun. His name is Ring.

A few such exercises as the above will, to use a common expression, get pupils in the way of writing compositions. It is frequently necessary to resort to such expedients to get pupils interested and started, after which they may become the best of writers. I have no doubt that the name *Composition* has frightened many a person who, by proper training, would have made a good writer.

The next easiest kind of composition is that of letter writing. Familiar letters to friends, giving an account of a party, a sleigh-ride, a picnic, a description of their homes or their school-house, telling what work they have done or what studies they are pursuing, or anything else which may interest them, may be written by pupils in a Grammar class. There will be no difficulty in getting the majority of pupils in such a class to try their skill at such work. There may be some who will refuse, either from diffidence or from stubbornness, to attempt anything of the kind, but by kind endeavor, by argument, they may be won over by the teacher.

The teacher should not be too severe in criticising compositions of beginners; rather praise than condemn, confining criticisms at first entirely to spelling, capitalization, grammatical errors and the more important parts of punctuation. As the pupil acquires more skill in the use of the pen in conveying thought the criticisms may extend to the matter of elegance, style, etc. After exercise in writing compositions from questions and in writing letters of friendship, easy descriptions may be attempted. The following outline and essay on "Stoves" will be suggestive of this kind of exercise:

Stove.
  Definition.
    Parts.
      Top.
      Bottom.
      Sides.
      Doors.
        Body.
        Hinges.
      Lids.
      Ovens.
      Water reservoir.
      Hearth.
      Dampers.
      Pipe.
      Flues.
      Ash pan.
      Mica doors.
      Grate.

Kinds.
  With regard to use:
    Cooking.
    Heating.
  With regard to shape:
    Box.
    Cannon.
    Plain.
    Ornamental.
  With regard to fuel:
    Wood.
    Coal.
    Gas.
    Oil.

STOVES.

A stove is an iron box, arranged in such a manner that a fire can be made in it and the smoke and gas conducted out of the room, and is used for the purpose of heating rooms and for cooking food, etc.

Some stoves have a flat top with holes, which are covered with lids, for the purpose of cooking, heating water, etc. Others have round or irregular shaped tops, made more for ornament than for use. The sides are generally ornamented with raised designs. Some are provided with ovens for baking purposes. Under the oven there are flues for conducting the heated air. In front there is a receptacle for ashes called the hearth, containing sometimes a pan to hold the ashes, which can be lifted out and emptied when full. An arrangement is made in the flue or pipe to open or shut, to regulate the draft. It is called a damper. Stoves for burning coal have grates to hold the coal up, so that the ashes will separate. All stoves have doors with hinges. Sometimes these doors have little windows with a transparent mineral called mica in them, instead of glass. Glass could not be used, as the heat would crack it. These little windows make a stove look very pretty, as through them we can see the glowing fire. I like to sit and look at the bright, glowing coals.

There are many kinds of stoves. We may divide them into kinds with regard to use, as cooking stoves and heating stoves, or with regard to shape and style, as box, cannon, plain and ornamental stoves; also with regard to the fuel used, as wood, coal, oil and gas stoves. Some stoves are very pretty pieces of furniture, and cost a great deal of money.

There are many familiar objects which would be much easier to describe than a stove. I have given this as an example of what may be done by almost any pupil old enough to use a text-book in Grammar. Many pupils could write a far better description than the one given above. The teacher should make suggestions upon the outline, giving facts which the pupil may not be possessed of and hints in regard to describing the different parts. The points in the above outline may be drawn from the class by judicious questioning. These essays need not be long. Better write short compositions, and have them well written, than long ones badly composed.

I have found that children, and indeed all of us, do not lack so much for language as we do for ideas, or rather ideas in a classified and connected form. This exercise of outlining furnishes a means of arranging our ideas in a proper shape so that we can write or speak of one thing at a time and in a proper order. In this way we need not repeat nor omit anything, for the plan and order of what we are going to say is mapped out for us. One will indeed be astonished at his own knowledge when he sees it thus arranged and spread out before him.

After exercises in easy description, subjects in simple narration may be given. Let the pupils narrate what they did during the previous day or week. In the lives of the humblest individuals enough transpires almost every day, if all the minutiæ were written, to make quite a lengthy composition. Any one can certainly say more than Mark Twain said in his diary which he kept when a boy, viz: " Got up, washed and went to bed." This was all he could think of each day to write in his diary, so he kept repeating it day after day until it became tiresome, and he abandoned the idea of keeping a diary. Let a pupil narrate all the actions in order as he can call them to mind, from getting up in'the morning to going to bed at night. For example, let me enumerate some of the actions of a boy during one day: Got up, washed his face, combed his hair, ate his breakfast (here I might enumerate the different articles of food eaten, tell some things that were said at the table, etc.), carried in wood, chopped wood, fed the horses, cows, sheep and pigs, carried water, went to a neighbor's on an errand, started to school, met some other boys, played awhile on the road, was late to school, studied and recited the various lessons (here I might tell some things that he learned), played certain games at noon and recess, came home, did the chores, which I need not enumerate, being the same as he did in the morning, ate supper and went to bed. Have I omitted anything? Yes, I did not say he ate dinner. Now, let a boy tell all this in his own way, subject to the criticisms of his classmates and teacher, and he will have quite a little piece of narration, and the foundation may be laid for a future journalist. Let the pupils give an account of some accident which happened in the neighborhood, or of a quarrel which took place on the play-ground, or an account of a trip to some town, river or lake, or an account of an excursion, a picnic, or a visit to a factory or foundry.

This essay writing should be given in connection with a review of the points of technical Grammar, and need not be a daily exercise. Perhaps about two days out of the week may be profitably devoted to this; the other three to written and oral lessons in parsing and analysis. This matter will, however, vary with circumstances. The teacher must be the judge.

Grammar need not be considered a dry, hard study if it is properly taught. As before stated, there should be but one class in Grammar in a country school, but that class should have, on an average, seven or eight pupils, instead of two or three, as is the case in schools which have come under my observation.

I append a few models for the written parsing of the parts of speech, as being suggestive to the teacher:

NOUN.

John studies grammar.

John, n., prop., masc., third, sing., nom., subj. of the prop., John studies grammar. R. The subject of a proposition, etc.

PRONOUN.

I bought the book.

I, pron., pers., simp., antec., name of the person speaking, masc., first, sing., R. [Here give rule for agreement.] nom., subj. of the prop., I bought the book. R. [Here give rule for construction.]

I remember what you said.

What, pron., rel., equivalent to *that which*, *that* being the *antec.* part and *which* the *relative*.

That, adj., pronom., used as a noun, obj., object of v. remember.

Which, pron., rel., antec. *that*, neut., third, sing., obj., object of v. said. R.

VERB.

Liberty is sweet.

Is, v., irreg. (am, was, being, been,) intrans., indic., pres., third, sing., agrees with subj. *liberty*. R.

ADVERB.

He acted wisely.

Wisely, adv. (comp. wisely, more wisely, most wisely,) of manner, modifies v. *acted*. R.

ADJECTIVE.

The diligent boy will be praised.

Diligent, adj., descrip., com., (comp. diligent, more diligent, most diligent) pos. qualifies n. *boy*.

CHAPTER VI.

HISTORY.

History is one of the most important of studies, yet I venture to say of those who have considerable knowledge of history, that they did not obtain much of it in school. History is a narration of events. No one has a memory sufficient to retain all events which have been made known to him. The great mistake made by too many teachers is, that they try to teach History in detail, and the pupils, in trying to remember all, remember but little. It is like trying to take up a dozen eggs at once in one hand. In the endeavor to grasp all we get none. Could we, indeed, remember all the details of History, of what benefit would it be? It is only the great events and the lessons to be drawn from them which are of benefit to us. I remember studying History in a country school, years ago. We read a lesson over and the teacher asked us all the questions found at the bottom of the page. We answered many of them and generally in the language of the author. The teacher pronounced us good scholars, but to-day I can scarcely recall a single event learned from that book. I distinctly remember the portraits of Washington and Daniel Webster, miserable wood cuts, that had, I suppose, a faint resemblance to the shadows of those great men, also a picture representing the death of General Wolfe, and that the book was bound in black cloth and had red edges, and that is about all I can remember. I have since then taken considerable interest in reading History in course; but I can say that I learned far more that has been of real benefit to me by teaching it, and my success I ascribe to the fact that I tried to select a few of the most important events and their dates to fix in the minds of my pupils, and in doing so, I learned them myself.

The greater number of the text-books on History used in our schools are failures, even in the hands of good teachers. Why? Because they are but masses of dry details. Why not give only the most important events and illustrate them by anecdote and by a felicitous mode of relating them, rather than catalogue-like paragraphs, giving only the dry bones or chronology of the subject. There may be others, but thus far I have seen but one book which meets my ideas of a good school History. It is Barnes' Brief History of the United States, published by A. S. Barnes & Co., New York and Chicago. If the teacher have not such a work he should have half a dozen different authors and be well read in different works, that he may, when he has selected the important points, so illustrate them that pupils will remember them in spite of themselves.

The main point in learning History is to make many minor events cluster and crystallize around some important fact which should be learned as thoroughly as the multiplication table. The association of ideas aids much in the study of History. Why do we all remember who General Greene was? Because he figured in the Revolution, and that is one of the events which will be remembered the easiest by all readers of History. So, when we think of the Revolution, we think of a hundred other things more or less directly connected with it.

The best way probably to teach history is to require the pupils to write essays on historical subjects, but this is impracticable in country schools. The next best plan is to assign each pupil a topic for investigation and report. A lesson of considerable length may be assigned the class, dividing it up into portions, giving each pupil a certain subject to investigate especially, but expecting him to read the whole lesson over several times carefully. Certain portions of the lesson may be read at recitation, the same as in a reading class; then each pupil is required to report on his topic, others criticising and adding to it if possible. In this way the whole lesson may be brought out, and by class drill on the most important parts, and by daily reviews, a pretty thorough knowledge of the whole subject may be obtained. The most important parts should be reviewed until fixed, and then the lesser details may be taken up. Remembering dates is not the whole of studying history, but it is an important part of it. Some persons have a much better memory of dates than others. I would have a class remember a few important dates first, and gradually add to them until I had all the dates of importance. The teacher should write on the board two columns of dates; one in large characters the other in small. Among the large characters he may put 1492, 1565, 1607, 1620, 1754, 1776, etc. The events connected with these dates may be first studied, each one made a lesson. As the lesser points are brought out the dates may be placed in the second column. Reviews should be had daily until each member of the class can relate the event connected with the dates in the first column; then the dates in the second column should be reviewed until they are learned. A few only may be placed in the second column, and a third column of still lesser dates be made. The point is to learn the most important first, and then those of less importance, and so on as many as are likely to be permanently remembered.

Instead of keeping a class a whole term on a few pages of the history of the United States, in order to learn all the minutiæ, I would take them through the book and let them gather what they could, taking care that it would be the prominent facts first, and then as much more as possible. But I would not be understood as taking them through the history as through a chronological table, getting only the dry bones, but I would clothe these with living, breathing flesh as I went along. A certain amount of detail is necessary to illustrate and make an important fact interesting, yet the detail should be used to help fix the main fact in the mind. To make my point plainer, suppose the subject to be the French and Indian wars. Now, there were numerous battles and skirmishes and treaties, but before I would expect a class to remember them all I would have them read an interesting account of Braddock's defeat and the fall of Quebec, the two most prominent events in all those wars. I would have them know something of the character and conduct of Braddock, the discipline of British soldiers, the mode of fighting among the Indians, the locality of the battle, the career of the young Washington, etc., and in the other case the death of Wolfe and Montcalm and all the circumstances connected with it, the nature of the battle-ground, etc. Two lessons might be given which would make a more permanent impression, and two dates learned which would be longer remembered than if a dozen lessons had been made of this subject and all the dates and minor details of these wars committed to memory.

To make the study interesting, and for variety, the teacher should gather together, for the purpose of using in his class, a number of the characteristic sayings of historical characters, as "Don't give up the ship;" "We have met the enemy and they are ours;" "A little more grape, Capt. Bragg;" "We will fight it out on this line if it takes all summer," etc.; also some of the popular appellations of great men, as "Rough and Ready," "Sage of Monticello," "The American Pathfinder," etc., and such terms as "Fillibusters," "Know Nothings," "Grangers." He can make use of this list in review lessons, and it will add much to the interest of the recitation. By use of judicious questions the teacher can, in reviewing, fix many points of interest. Questions somewhat as follows should be asked: Who was Roger Williams? Pocahontas? Sir Walter Raleigh? Balboa? Major

Andre? etc. What men figured prominently in the war of 1812? What battle was fought after peace was declared between the two countries? What led to the settlement of California? What were the acquisitions of territory to the United States? Who was President during the war of 1812? During the Mexican war? What was the Missouri Compromise? etc. A few such questions should be asked for review every day.

Pupils who are sufficiently advanced and have time from other studies, should be encouraged to write short sketches on historical subjects. I would not impose it as a duty, but request it and encourage any inclination the pupil may show in that direction. They may be encouraged also to relate incidents which they may have read in other works.

There is no branch of learning in which there is such susceptibility of illustration by the introduction of collateral and explanatory matter. If the teacher be well read he can enliven each recitation by relating briefly some incident or making some explanation not found in the text-books.

The study of Geography should go hand in hand with History. Free use of the map and globe should be made to illustrate the lessons. Pupils should be encouraged to read fragments of History, such as Abbott's Histories, some of the more interesting biographies of great men, and many of the historical works written especially for the young. The teacher should point out certain such works which may be accessible to his pupils.

Attention should be paid to the progress and development of science, art and literature among the people; and in reviews scientific men, inventors, artists, poets and authors should be grouped according to their respective epochs. The dates of great inventions and discoveries and their effects on civilization should be remembered, as well as the rise and fall of dynasties or the record of battles and political intrigues.

CHAPTER VII.

ANATOMY, PHYSIOLOGY AND HYGIENE.

Anatomy, teaching the structure of our bodies; Physiology, the functions of the various organs; and Hygiene, the application of this knowledge to the maintaining of a sound mind in a sound body, are subjects usually included under the term Physiology, and are required by law, in many of the States, to be taught in common schools, or rather the teacher is required to be prepared to teach them. It is eminently proper that this subject should be taught in country schools.

Notwithstanding the fact that an out-door life of labor is more conducive to health and longevity than a sedentary in-door life, country people need the knowledge, which, if properly applied, will conserve their health and bodily vigor. Farmers do not always obey the laws of health in regard to diet and exercise, and farmers' children need instruction on this point as well as in regard to keeping accounts or any other branch taught in schools.

The teacher will find that the same methods of teaching which are applicable in Geography, Grammar and History can be successfully applied in this branch. The topic method should prevail, and pupils should be encouraged to outline and classify the subjects treated in the text-book. A class can be perhaps more successfully conducted if each pupil has a different author in his hands than if they all had the same. The truly alive teacher will find no difficulty in presenting the subject and conducting a recitation, but questions of more importance are these: What parts shall be studied, and where shall the class commence? The subject is too deep to be studied in detail by pupils of a country school. Only the more important general principles should be taught, and these well impressed upon their minds. The following are some of the points which the teacher should select and the order in which they should be presented:

I. GENERAL FRAMEWORK OF THE BODY.

1. *Bones.*

Let the class make out an outline of the bones, naming every bone in the body under the main divisions of Head, Trunk and Extremities, then proceed to learn the names of a few of the more important bones first; those of less importance may be learned incidentally by reviews and class drills. Next give a lesson or two on the structure and use of the bones and their importance in a hygienic sense, as, for example, the importance of recognizing the fact that children's bones are softer and contain less mineral matter, and the bones of old persons are in the opposite conditions, and make the application as regards managing children to prevent bow legs, spinal deformities, etc., and care to prevent accidents causing fracture in elderly persons. Three or four lessons will thus bring out all the more important matters relating to the bones. By frequent reviews, after the pupil has advanced to other subjects, these important facts will be fixed in their memories and seen in their relations to other facts of the science. You must proceed according to the intellectual calibre of your pupils. If they are capable of grasping the more abstruse parts, lead them gradually into them; if not, teach what they can comprehend and teach that well.

2. *Muscles.*

Make outlines as with the bones, naming those muscles usually given in school text-books, and memorizing a few of the more important. The teacher may give hints in regard to the outline, suggesting that the structure, arrangement, kinds and use of muscles form a part of the outline. Several lessons are then to be made on these points.

3. *The Skin.*

A lesson or two on this subject, discussing its structure and use, including hair and nails, mucous membrane and teeth, the three latter being modifications of the epidermis, or outer skin. The functions of the skin will be better understood after the subject of respiration, digestion and circulation are studied.

The whole subject of the framework of the body may now be reviewed by outlines and general questions and discussions.

II. VITAL PROCESSES.

1. *Digestion.*

Make out outlines of the organs of digestion, including teeth, tongue, salivary glands, œsophagus, stomach, intestinal canal, pancreas and liver. Describe these parts in a general manner, and next outline and describe the processes of digestion, as mastication, insalivation, deglutition, chymification, chylification, with the fluids necessary to perform these processes, as saliva, gastric juice, bile and pancreatic fluid. Tell what processes are mechanical and what chemico-vital. A number of lessons should be made of the subject of digestion, as it is of great importance. Give a lesson on the hygiene of digestion in relation to manner and matter of diet.

2. *Circulation.*

Outline organs, as arteries, veins, capillaries, heart, lymphatics, with a discussion of the processes and results. Drill particularly in tracing the course of the blood in the round of the circulation. Draw diagram on blackboard to illustrate.

3. *Respiration.*

Outline and discuss organs, as trachea, bronchial tubes, lungs, air cells, capillaries, with processes and results, as elimination of impurities and production of pure blood for vital purposes. Show the relation between the lungs and skin in the processes of excretion. Explain the philosophy of "taking cold" and the necessity of good ventilation.

Review the whole subject of vital processes and dwell on the hygiene of digestion, as it may now be better understood after a discussion of circulation and respiration. A general review from the beginning may now be given, asking questions which will make pupils think and reason, and drill on the more important parts to fix them in the memory.

III. NERVOUS SYSTEM.

The structure, functions and hygiene of the nervous system should be studied by outlines, making the grand divisions of cerebro-spinal and sympathetic systems, also bringing in the terms sensory and motor nerves. I need not explain here further, as the teacher who has conducted a class properly thus far will understand how to present this subject.

II. THE SPECIAL SENSES.

The eye and ear should be studied in considerable detail, paying particular attention to the *hygiene* of these organs. A little knowledge of the sciences of optics and acoustics would be of benefit to the teacher Let him study these subjects in some work on natural philosophy, and he will be better able to explain the functions of these organs.

If the class is capable of going farther during one term, there are many other points which may be taken up and discussed, but first let a thorough investigation of the points I have noted be made. I insist on frequent reviews. The teacher, at least, should have more than one text-book, and it would be well if the class had different authors also. There are some very good text-books on the subject designed for common schools. Among them may be mentioned Steeles' and Cutter's. Some of the review questions in "Steele's Fourteen Weeks" are valuable aids to the teacher. If his class has not that book he should use some of those questions by writing them on the board for review lessons. The teacher should use all possible aids in illustrating the anatomy of important organs. It is possible to procure specimens from animals which will illustrate many points in the human system. The eye of a hog is about the same in size and structure as the human eye, and specimens should be procured and dissected before the class. If one is boiled it will bear dissection better, but it should be shown also in a natural state. The larynx of a hog will also illustrate the human larynx, and give a much clearer idea than pictures or models. In fact nearly all the internal organs of the hog are similar in size and appearance to those of the human being. The heart, lungs and stomach, even, of a hog may be exhibited to illustrate these parts in the human body. Bones of animals may be procured and sawn across to show the structure. Five cents worth of sulphuric acid, to be had at any drug store, will, if diluted, dissolve the earthy parts of bone, leaving the animal parts intact. A bone may be burned in the stove, destroying the animal part and leaving the earthy part.

CHAPTER VIII.

ALGEBRA AND THE HIGHER MATHEMATICS.

The science of Algebra is taught regularly in many of our country schools, and some portions of the Higher Mathematics, as Geometry, Trigonometry, Astronomy, etc., should be taught incidentally in connection with other branches and occasionally by regular lessons, although without using a regular text-book.

Algebra is a method of solving mathematical problems and representing quantities by means of symbols. It is an indispensable aid in all the higher mathematical branches. It is sometimes called General Arithmetic, and as an aid to Arithmetic it is of great value. It should be studied before Arithmetic is finished. It frequently happens that the teacher finds an example in Arithmetic which will at first puzzle him, and very often a knowledge of Algebra will help him out of the difficulty. He may solve the example by Algebra, and from this get an arithmetical solution. As merely an aid to the teacher, even if he is never required to teach it, it is valuable.

It will appear evident that Algebra should be taught very much the same as Arithmetic. I will therefore only offer a few suggestions:

There are a certain number of definitions which must be learned before much progress can be made, but I would not advise a study of them alone. The teacher should first develop the algebraic idea of representing quantities by symbols. Take, for example, the sum of 24 and 32. Instead of adding the numbers, as in Arithmetic, you will say, "we will represent the number 24 by a, and the number 32 by b, and the operation will then stand $a+b$." Some of the simple examples in Arithmetic should be presented and solved algebraically. For instance, such problems as the following:

"A travels a certain distance one day and twice as far the next. In the two days he travels 36 miles; how far does he travel each day?"

A number of such examples should be solved by the pupils before definitions should be learned. A few definitions only are necessary at first; the others to be learned as the necessity arises for their use.

Numerous examples, like the following, may be given while the pupil is learning the necessary definitions:

"What is the value of $c+d-b$, c being equal to 5, d to 10 and b to 3?"

As soon as the pupil is somewhat familiar with algebraic forms of expression, the operations of addition, subtraction, multiplication and division of algebraic quantities should be taught, giving numerous examples for practice, and requiring pupils to be particular in the use of signs.

Be sure that all pupils have the proper conception of adding and subtracting algebraic quantities and of the idea that letters may represent *any* quantity. With these facts well impressed and clearly understood, there will be no difficulty in conducting a class successfully through any text-book on the science, if the teacher has profited by the hints on teaching Arithmetic.

I have already spoken of some of the applications of the higher mathematics in the chapter on Arithmetic. With advanced pupils in Algebra or Arithmetic a slight knowledge of Geometry and Trigonometry may be taught if the teacher has prepared himself by the study of these branches. For example, even very young pupils can be taught the meaning of many geometrical terms, as angle, plane, the different kinds of triangles, perpendicular, diagonal, parallel lines, parts of a circle, chords, polygons, prisms, etc., and advanced pupils in country schools should certainly be made familiar with these terms. Some of the simpler propositions may be demonstrated, or at least taught as facts. The blocks before spoken of (see p. 50), and which should be in every school-room, will aid in familiarizing pupils with geometrical terms. The process of finding distances by similar triangles and some other parts of Trigonometry may be taught. School boys are sometimes curious to know how astronomers can tell the distance of the sun from the earth. This may be made plain to them by a simple calculation. For a solution of this problem, see April number, 1879, of Normal Teacher. Many of the facts of mathematical Geography may also be made plainer by a knowledge of geometrical forms and principles.

I will close this chapter by saying, do not be bound within the narrow limits of the text-book your class is using, but wherever you can fix a fact or draw out a demonstration in any useful line of investigation do so, but do not waste time in trying to demonstrate what your pupils are not old enough, or have not the intellectual power to understand; and above all things do not try to demonstrate anything you do not yourself understand. If you are asked a question, or to explain something of which you are ignorant, do not pretend to know or put them off with an excuse, but frankly acknowledge your ignorance; then study on that point until you have mastered it, if it be possible.

CHAPTER IX.

THE NATURAL SCIENCES.

Under this head I wish to discuss the teaching of Botany, Geology, Natural Philosophy, Chemistry and Zoology in country schools. I think I hear some one saying, "What! do you propose that all these branches be taught in our common country schools?" I answer such a person by saying, "Yes; not regularly, not necessarily with text-books, but incidentally and occasionally as a means of culture and for the purpose of keeping up interest, enthusiasm, assisting in governing, and with the hope that some good seeds may be sown which will find proper soil and receive a start which may culminate in a future Agassiz or Linnæus." "But teachers are not generally prepared to teach such subjects. They have no knowledge of them themselves." Then they should go to work and inform themselves.

Children will often take a deep interest in collecting specimens and exhibit a strong desire to know something about them. There is much difference in neighborhoods in this respect. There are some backwoods communities where anything of the kind would be looked upon as the utmost degree of foolishness, and the people would be ready to call the teacher who would attempt anything of the kind a lunatic. The teacher, then, must first feel the public pulse, and beware how he carries innovations into the school-room. Wherever anything of the kind is entirely new the teacher must proceed with caution, and make gradual advances until he captures the fort.

1. Let us see what the teacher may do in the line of botanical teaching. If it is in the spring, summer or fall, he may procure a few leaves of different kinds, and either at general exercise, or during the five minutes intervals of rest, call the attention of the school to them. Show them that in one sense they are all alike, and in another all different; that is, they all have a midrib and branching veins. You may draw this fact out by asking questions. You may ask them in what respect they are all alike. They will probably say they are all green. Then you may ask them if any of them ever saw a leaf that was not green. They will probably answer, no. You may tell them that nearly all leaves are green, but there are some leaves that are colored, or partly so. Tell them to ask their parents if they ever saw a leaf that was not green when young and growing. You may call for a report the next day. Ask them in what respect the leaves are different. They will answer at once that they are of different shapes. You may now close the exercise for this time by telling them that to-morrow you want to see how many different shaped leaves each one can bring. You may make a collection of leaves. Dry them by laying between folds of paper. If pupils take an interest in making a collection (which I am sure they will,

many of them at least), you may give a number of lessons on the leaf, classifying them according to their shape. An outline may be written on the blackboard, and though it will bring in some new words with which the pupils are not familiar, the words are not difficult of comprehension when explained; besides you need not use the technical term when a common word will answer. The words of the outline can be used as a spelling lesson for the next day. I give below a specimen of an outline which may be made out on the subject of leaves:

Leaves.
1. Parts.
    1. Blade.
        1. Midrib.
        2. Veins.
    2. Foot stalk or leaf stalk.
2. Forms.
    1. As to general outline.
        1. Linear.
        2. Lance-shaped.
        3. Oblong.
        4. Elliptical.
        5. Oval.
        6. Ovate.
        7. Orbicular or rotund.
        8. Oblanceolate.
        9. Wedge-shaped.
        10. Spoon-shaped.
        11. Obovate.

2. As to base.
   1. Heart-shaped.
   2. Kidney-shaped.
   3. Eared.
   4. Arrow-shaped.
   5. Halberd-shaped.
   6. Shield-shaped.
3. As to Apex.
   1. Pointed.
   2. Acute.
   3. Obtuse.
   4. Truncate.
   5. Retuse.
   6. Notched.
   7. Obcordate.
   8. Tooth-shaped.
   9. Mucronate.
   10. Bristle-pointed.
4. As to particular outline.
   1. Entire.
   2. Saw-toothed.
   3. Toothed.
   4. Scalloped.
   5. Wavy.
   6. Sinuate.
   7. Cut or jagged.
   8. Lobed.
   9. Cleft.
   10. Parted.
   11. Divided.
   12. Simple.
   13. Compound.
       1. Pinnate.
       2. Palmate.

A couple of weeks may be profitably and pleasantly spent studying the subject of leaves in this way, using no more than five minutes each day. It will be easy enough to collect specimens to represent nearly all the above forms of leaves, and as the pupils do this work at noons and recesses and mornings and evenings, but little time is consumed, much interest can be awakened, some knowledge imparted, and, without a doubt, some dormant mind will be aroused and the perceptive faculties cultivated.

If in winter, a collection of the different kinds of wood may be made by the pupils. This may be made very interesting. The teacher should specify the size and shape of the blocks. They should be cut so as to show the grain of the wood, both longitudinal and transverse, with one side and one end planed or polished. They should then be correctly and plainly labelled and kept as a part of the property of the school. Those kinds which are native of the country should be so designated, and those which are foreign. In this way a complete collection of all the native woods of the locality and many of foreign species may be made, and will be a collection of value when complete. The teacher may give some very interesting lectures on the uses, strength, etc., of woods. The pupils may be asked to name some of the uses of wood, what kinds of wood are valuable for certain purposes, etc. The teacher may procure specimens of foreign woods, as lignumvitæ, logwood, ebony, etc., and speak of their uses in the arts and their value in a commercial sense.

There is not a locality in the United States where such exercises as the above can not be made practical, a statement which can not be made in regard to Geological teaching. The live teacher may find other practical and profitable exercises touching the science of Botany, but these, it is hoped, are sufficient as hints.

2. In many localities Geology may be made a profitable study, and a collection of specimens of fossils and minerals be made. There are localities where fossils are numerous, and there are but few places where there are not different kinds of rocks. Let a collection be commenced and extended as far as possible, even if the locality is poor in specimens. The teacher should endeavor to inform himself on the subject of Geology, that he may be able to answer the numerous queries which may be put to him in regard to rocks, minerals and fossils. Interesting short lectures may be given upon rocks, ores, fossils, etc. Let the teacher prepare himself by reading and study for a short talk about some of these subjects. I have not space to suggest what he may say, but can only, in a general way, hint that he endeavor to make these talks interesting by talking about what the pupils seem to take an interest in. The grand object is to make up mind. When a thirst for knowledge is once induced it is easy to supply the demand. By a few judicious questions and statements, the teacher will find out what he can talk about with the greatest degree of success. The teacher should, if possible, procure specimens of the different kinds of coal, of iron, lead, zinc and copper ores, of gold and silver-bearing quartz, of granite, marble, sand-stone, chalk, slate, etc. In localities where there are no such things, they will be a source of interest to the whole school and to Geography classes in particular. A Geological collection of such representative specimens should

form a part of the teacher's stock in trade. He may procure them in his travels and through the medium of friends and by exchange with others interested in the same subjects.

3. Some very interesting experiments in Natural Philosophy and Chemistry may be performed by the teacher, and the principles made plain to pupils. In searching a work on these subjects you will find many experiments described which, with a little modification, you may perform with little or no cost for apparatus or material. Much of the apparatus for performing experiments in Natural Philosophy and Chemistry may be devised by any teacher who has ordinary ingenuity. These subjects will not, perhaps, be so well adapted to the whole school as Botany and Geology, but with classes in Physiology and advanced Geography, many experiments may be performed and principles illustrated which will prove of great use in widening their field of knowledge and stimulating them to independent investigation and research. I remember, when quite a small boy, I read "Parker's Philosophy" and performed several of the experiments there described without ever consulting any one. I found a crooked stem of a poke-weed, and pushing out the pith, made a syphon, and got a scolding for running the water out of my mother's rain-water barrel. Boys frequently exhibit such tendencies at a very early age. A horse-shoe magnet may be purchased for a few cents, and many wonderful experiments performed with it, illustrating the properties of that mysterious agent, electricity. If some common bituminous coal be reduced to a powder and

heated in the bowl of a clay tobacco pipe, by covering with moistened clay, the gas which is developed may be burned at the end of the pipe stem. It is the common illuminating gas which lights our cities. If a little lump of green vitriol be dropped into a glass of clear water it will dissolve, and the solution will be clear. Now, if a solution of tannic acid be made, either by dropping a very small quantity into another glass of water, or a few drops of tea from oak bark be added to the water, and the contents of one glass be mixed with the contents of the other, the two previously clear solutions will turn instantly black as ink. Here is an illustration of a chemical change. I will give another just as simple. Drop a small particle of starch in a glass of hot water. Into another glass put a drop of tincture of iodine. The clear liquids, when mixed, will assume a beautiful blue color. Here is one of a different character: Mix a teaspoonful of chlorate of potash with a similar quantity of sugar; lay on a board and let fall a single drop of sulphuric acid (oil of vitriol) upon it. The mass will take fire and burn with a beautiful white flame and with great rapidity. A volcano may be illustrated with this material. Raise a pile of earth on a wide board, and in the center place a little of this material wrapped in paper, arranging a paper tube so as to reach the apex of the volcano and communicate with the material inside. Let fall a drop of the acid through this tube, and instantly the volcano will have an eruption, belching forth fire and smoke. Although the teacher may not be able to explain the exact nature of these chemical changes, the purpose is served as well. It is only necessary to show that a new and different substance is produced by a chemical reaction. The pupil may be referred to the process of making soap from fats and alkalies as an illustration of a chemical change producing a new substance.

I have had for a number of years in contemplation a small book of easy experiments in chemistry and philosophy, and part of the manuscript is already prepared. It would contain a vast number of simple and easy experiments illustrating important points. I have placed it in the hands of other parties, and no doubt it will be finished and issued from the press at no distant day. Such a work will, I have no doubt, be of immense value to the teacher, both as an aid to the study of these sciences, and as a valuable help in the school-room.

4. A few words in regard to the teaching of Natural History in the country school. Here is a wide field for youth to investigate, but the country teacher will not find it so available as the foregoing sciences. Specimens can not be collected unless it be in the department of insects. If any teacher's taste incline in that direction perhaps he may make this branch a profitable one. Children love to hear and read about animals. Stories of animal sagacity may be related, and questions asked about the animals of different countries, their habits, uses, etc. Pupils may be told, for example, of the reindeer, an animal which furnishes food, drink, clothing, shelter and implements for a certain class of people; of some of the articles of commerce which are produced from animals, as

ivory, bone, whalebone, oil, leather, horn, glue, furs, wool, feathers, etc.; of the animals peculiar to different parts of the world, etc. Some of these points belong to Geography, but may be taught to the whole school as general exercises.

CHAPTER X.

MORALS AND MANNERS.

A grave responsibility rests upon the teacher. He should do vastly more than the law requires of him or his employers expect of him. Instructing children in the branches treated of in text-books is not the only teaching a teacher should do. There is something higher and nobler for him to do. He must teach lessons in morals and manners, the substratum on which a free government rests. Let me here make an extract from Prof. Huxley's address before the Johns Hopkins University:

"Size is not grandeur, and territory does not make a nation. The great issue about which hangs a true sublimity, and the terror of overhanging fate is, what are you going to with all these things? What is to be the end to which these are to be the means? You are making a novel experiment in politics on the greatest scale which the world has yet seen. Forty millions at your first centenary! It is reasonably to be expected that at the second, these States will be occupied by two hundred millions of English speaking people spread over an area as large as that of Europe, and with climates and interests as diverse as those of Spain and Scandinavia, England and Russia.

You and your descendants have to ascertain whether this great mass will hold together under the forms of a republic and the despotic reality of universal suffrage; whether State rights will hold out against centralization without separation; whether centralization will get the better without actual or disguised monarchy; whether shifting corruption is better than a permanent bureaucracy; and as population thickens in your cities and the pressure of want is felt, the gaunt spectre of pauperism will stalk among you and communism and socialism will claim to be heard. Truly America has a great future before her; great in toil, in care and in responsibility; great in true glory, if she be guided in wisdom and righteousness; great in shame, if she fail. I can not understand why other nations should envy you, or be blind to the fact that it is for the highest interest of mankind that you should succeed; *but the one condition of success, your sole safeguard, is the moral worth and intellectual clearness of the individual citizen.* Education can not give these, but it may cherish them and bring them to the front in whatever station of society they are to be found, and the universities ought to be and may be the fortresses of the higher life of the nation."

I would agree with Huxley in all but the last sentence. Education *can* give *moral worth and intellectual clearness*, and the *common schools*, and especially the *country district schools*, " ought to be and may be the fortresses of the higher life of the nation." How many of our great men were educated in our country schools? Many received their first impulses in some log school-house in the back-woods. The country school teacher has given an impetus to the intellectual development of many a statesman and man of worth to the nation. He has made many a man capable of casting an intelligent ballot, and has he not increased the moral worth of many a citizen of this great republic? Much more can he do if guided by right motives and prompted to greater zeal by a true understanding of the responsibility of his position and a real love for the profession. Hear what one of our greatest statesmen, Daniel Webster, said about the common school: "Many moral tales and instructive and well contrived fables, always so alluring to children, learned by heart in these schools, are still perfectly preserved in my memory. * * * In my opinion, the instruction communicated in the free schools of New England has a direct effect for good on the morals of youth. It represses vicious inclinations, it inspires love of character and it awakens honorable aspirations."

The teacher should endeavor by every means in his power to instill into his pupils habits which will make them good citizens of a free republic. The following outline will indicate the order in which I propose a very brief notice of some of the points which teachers should take pains to teach, both by precept and example:

1. Morals.
    1. Veracity.
        1. Avoid Lying.
        2. Avoid Deception.
    2. Honesty.
        1. Avoid Theft.
        2. Avoid Cheating.
    3. Industry.
        1. At Study.
        2. At Work.
    4. Economy.
        1. Save Property.
        2. Save Time.
    5. Promptness and Regularity.
        1. Regular in Attendance.
        2. Prompt at Recitations.
        3. Prompt in the Affairs of Life.
2. Manners.
    1. Politeness.
        1. To Strangers.
        2. To Teacher.
        3. To Companions.
    2. Respect.
        1. For Self.
        2. For Rights, Property and Persons of Others.
    3. Kindness.
        1. To Human Beings.
        2. To Animals.
    4. Generosity.
        1. In Yielding Rights and Privileges.
        2. In Giving and Sharing Property.
    5. Reverence.
        1. For God.
        2. For Parents.
        3. For Teachers.
        4. For Age.
    6. Purity of Speech.
        1. Avoid Swearing.
        2. Avoid Impure Language.

I. MORALS.

1. *Veracity*.—I need not enlarge on the necessity of inculcating in the young a sincere love of truth. Whenever possible the teacher should point out the evil effects of lying and deception in a community. Gossiping and tale-bearing are very nearly akin to lying. Children should be taught this, and discouraged in any tendency exhibited in this direction. Something has happened on the play-ground, and some one comes and tells the teacher. Here is an opportunity to speak about this matter. Children should be taught that when they are called upon individually for evidence in regard to offenses committed they should respond with the "truth, the whole truth, and nothing but the truth," but that a spirit of tattling and meddling should always be avoided. They should be taught that a person can act a lie as well as speak it, and that all double dealing and deception should be abhorred. The teacher can teach much more by example. He should always be just what he appears to be, and make no promises which he does not intend to perform. Many teachers teach deception by not performing what they promise. If it happens that he has made a promise he is unable to perform he should be quick to state his reasons, and frankly acknowledge an error if he commits one.

2. *Honesty*.—I fear that in this free republic few men and women are strictly honest. I do not mean that they all steal, but humbugging and cheating are such *common* things that few are entirely innocent.

I have, however, taught schools where it was not safe to leave a pencil or knife on the table and leave the room, but it was because there was one thief in the school; I could not accuse the school of being dishonest. But children need cautioning about taking little things which they might not regard as stealing. They should be shown how taking an apple may lead to taking a knife, and this to something of more value, and so on until they land in the penitentiary. I would not, however, speak very often about stealing, certainly not at all unless something occurred to give occasion to speak about it, for it is never good to anticipate the commission of a crime by making mention of it. I say anticipate it, for I believe that often the mere calling of a crime to mind will prompt its commission. I have not space here to discuss this fact, but it is a fact in human nature. Cheating is sometimes practiced in games of childhood. The teacher should take pains to check the tendency at once, for a child who will cheat in a game is likely to cheat in business when a man. Honesty should be taught, not simply because it is the best policy, but because it is one of the noblest traits of human character.

3. *Industry.*—I have classed industry as a moral trait, for no man can be a moral man and at the same time an idler. It lies at the foundation of individual and national life, co-ordinate with honesty and veracity. Habits of industry must be taught in school as well as in the family. The teacher can do much towards fostering this trait by furnishing all with employment in the school-room and by occasionally prompting the

idle-inclined pupils. This prompting must not be done in a scolding manner, but pleasantly, by directing them towards an example to be solved, a point to be noticed in the lesson, a paragraph to be read over, a written exercise to be attended to, etc. Occasion should be taken to point out the benefits of industry in the world. In geography classes, when lessons are had on the productions of various countries, call attention to the fact that the wealth and beauty of a country depend on the industry of its inhabitants; the fine cities, buildings, works of art, etc., are the results of industry. In general exercises in natural science, the uses of certain articles, as iron, wood, etc., should be shown to be the result of the industry of man. Show that these substances in a state of nature would be of little or no use to man. Call attention to the fact that the farmers who are the most wealthy are generally so from industry and economy. These two traits can not, indeed, be separated.

4. *Economy.*—I come, naturally, to speak of this also as a moral trait. From the days when the Prodigal Son wasted his substance in riotous living, and was at last obliged to return to an economical parent for support, to the present day, those individuals who have practiced economy have stood foremost in the world's history as the wise ones who provide for the future by taking care of the present, and to whom the prodigal and wasteful must come at last begging. It is to be hoped that the financial depression which this country has just passed through will teach lessons of economy that will benefit the adults of the present generation at least. But the youth of our schools

should receive instruction in this branch, that they may not have to learn by dear experience in the future what many of us are learning to-day. About every fifteen years there is a financial crash in this country, and it is caused solely by the extravagance and wastefulness of the inhabitants.

Pupils should be taught economy in the use of property and in the use of time. When books are heedlessly torn or soiled, or school property destroyed the teacher will have occasion to preach a lesson of economy in the use of property. A programme of study and recitation economizes time, and the pupils should be made to see this and be prompted to systemize their study that they may save time. Habits of economy thus impressed in youth will often have great effect on character in after life. Pupils trained to study by plan, will be apt to work and study by system when they enter the active arena of life.

5. *Promptness and Regularity.*—Another moral trait which should be instilled into youth at an early age. Regular attendance at school should be shown as highly necessary to secure the benefits of school. The teacher should talk to parents on this subject and show them that it would be to their own interest to send their children regularly to school. If they are to keep their children at home half the time, that time should be consecutively and not a day now and then. Train them to be prompt to come in when the bell rings, prompt to come to the recitation, prompt to answer when called upon to recite. Pupils who are in the habit of straggling when the bell rings should be reminded of the fact by being detained a few min-

utes after the others are dismissed. They can see the justice of this punishment, for if they persist in disturbing the order of the school by coming in late and try to gain a few moments for play at the expense of the rest of the school, they should be compelled to make up this time while those who have been prompt are permitted to play.

II. MANNERS.

It is often remarked that the youth of the present day are not so polite and do not show that respect for superiors which characterized the youth of the preceding generation. "It was not so when I was young," is an expression often upon the lips of elderly persons. It is true, also, that the American people are more lacking in these qualities than the Old World inhabitants. This fact is owing to our free self-government, which fosters an independent spirit, the opposite of a fawning, cringing servility. While this independent spirit should not be crushed out, but rather encouraged, the youth should be taught true manners, which consist in treating fellow beings as having equal rights to "life, liberty and the pursuit of happiness."

(See p. 53.)

1. *Politeness.*—The teacher will find frequent opportunity to give instruction on the duty of being polite to strangers, to teachers, and to companions. School children frequently insult, or in various ways act impudently, towards strangers who may happen to pass the school-house during play hours. The teacher should

try to check any such conduct at once, and take the opportunity to give a lecture on politeness. Pupils fail sometimes to speak in a respectful manner to the teacher or to each other. The teacher should call attention to these points, and remind the pupil of his want of politeness. The teacher should always speak and act politely toward pupils wherever he may meet them, thus teaching by example.

2. *Respect.*—He who has no respect for himself will have none for others. There is a kind of pride which every one should possess. It is that pride which leads us to do unto others as we would have them do unto us. We should take pride in doing right, and thus have respect for ourselves by so conducting our manners as to give no offense to others. A respect for the rights, property and person of others is but obeying the Golden Rule, as well as obeying the laws of our land. Children should be taught by example and precept that others have rights which they should be bound to respect. School and other public property is too frequently the object of wanton destruction, or the subject for defacement with knives, pencils, etc. Will you find a school house that has been built one year in all this country that does not bear the marks of a pencil or pocket-knife to a greater or less extent? Children should be taught that the property belongs to their parents, to every one in the district, and that they have no more right to deface or destroy it than if it were their neighbor's. They should be made acquainted with the laws of the State in regard to such defilement. Something must be done to check this spirit

of vandalism, which seems to be gaining ground in this country, and I know of no better place to begin educating the people to better respect public property than in the district school.

3. *Kindness.*—Boys are sometimes cruel to their playmates, especially to those younger and weaker than themselves. The teacher should not only see that no one under his charge is imposed upon, but he should take such opportunities to inculcate a spirit of kindness, not only towards human beings, but towards the brute creation. Teach them that kindness is a wonderful power; that it will conquer where fear will not. Show them what influence they may possess over others, and over animals, by being kind to them.

4. *Generosity.*—It is unnecessary to enlarge upon this head. Examples will be easily found upon which to preach a lesson of generosity. You can not place a number of individuals together without it being necessary for the general welfare, that certain rights and privileges and property be yielded from one person to others. This quality is absolutely necessary to the existence of the social state. Even animals which are in the habit of living together yield to each other certain privileges and share each other's food.

5. *Reverence.*—This is closely allied to respect. In fact, all the points in the outline are mutually dependent and blend into each other. But we should teach that there is a kind and benevolent Father who watches over us, and has the universe in charge, and who rules with justice and equity, but whose ways are sometimes to us mysterious, and that we, his chil-

dren and subjects of his sovereign will, should reverence and obey him. This is a quality of true manners, to reverence an aknowledged superior power. Our earthly parents claim also our reverence. They who have watched over us from infancy, and provided for our future welfare, certainly can claim a respect which amounts to reverence. The commandment, "Honor thy father and mother," if universally obeyed, would be a mighty factor in reforming the human race. As the teacher stands in *loco parentis* for the time being, he also demands a respect which may be called reverence. While the teacher should be on familiar terms with his pupils, he should ever maintain his dignity, and teach pupils that on account of his position he demands a certain degree of reverence. A teacher will have but little control over pupils who have not this respect, and a respect which may be called reverence, unless he has it by fear, and he can teach but little who governs by fear. Age demands a sort of reverence from youth, so long, at least, as age is respectful.

6. *Purity of Speech.*—A gentleman may be known by his speech. The young of our day are, in many localities, very much addicted to the use of profanity. It is not strange, however; when they have teachers on every hand, when the parents and companions of the child constantly use profane language, it is not strange that the child learns it. It is the teacher's duty to teach them that it is wrong, that it is a violation of the moral code, as well as a gross violation of etiquette. The country is also full of slang, and our youth, from infancy, almost, speak in the language of

slang. While it is true that there are some expressions, generally called slang, which are very forcible, and might be used occasionally to afford variety and emphasis to our language, the constant use of such expressions is but a sign of weakness, and they lose their force by being wrongfully applied and too frequently used.

It is of little use to punish pupils for swearing. In nine cases out of ten, the offender is only confirmed in his habit. As soon as he gets out of hearing of the teacher he will very likely swear at him for having punished him. His only care will thenceforth be, not to keep from swearing, but to swear when the teacher does not hear it. The better way is to talk to the school about the habit and try to persuade them to abandon it. You take five minutes some day, and when you have the attention of the whole school, talk to them in this manner: Boys, I have noticed you often when playing, and sometimes I have heard some of you swear and use language which, it seems to me, you would not like to repeat now if I were to ask you. Now, I have no doubt you hear somebody swear almost every day of your lives, and you have learned when you hardly knew you were learning it, and perhaps some of you may think it is not wrong because many men swear. Did you never think that men do wrong as well as boys, and if we would try to do what is right in the world it will not do to copy after men and do everything they do. Some men will steal horses and commit murder. Do you think it would be right for you to do so because these men do? It is very likely that these men learned to swear when they were small boys like some of you, and it became such a habit that it was almost impossible to break it off. Now, let me tell you to try and not be a slave to any habit. It is not hard to form habits now when you are young, and not very hard to break off bad habits, not half as hard as when you get older. Now, let me ask you to quit this habit just as soon as you can. You will forget and say bad words before you think, but you must think and be on your guard. Now, how many will try to keep from swearing or using bad language? I mean those who have not been guilty as well as those who have. Hold up your hands, as many of you as will try to avoid it. Now, that you have promised to try, I hope you will try, and I do not expect to hear very much swearing again.

This kind of moral suasion will have a much more salutary effect than any kind of punishment could have.

In concluding this chapter, let me say with Milton, keep your pupils "stirred up with high hopes of living to be brave men and worthy patriots, dear to God and famous to all ages."

CHAPTER XI.

MODEL RECITATIONS.

ADVANCED GEOGRAPHY.

Subject of the lesson—State of Iowa.

[Pupils take their places at the recitation seats at call of teacher or tap of bell.]

NOTE.—Each pupil has a copy of the outline on p.—

Teacher—John, can you step to the black-board and draw an outline map of Iowa, marking the principal points of interest?

John—I will try, Sir.

Teacher—Henry, you may tell us what you can about the position of Iowa.

Henry—It lies between Latitude $40\frac{1}{2}°$ and $43\frac{1}{2}°$ N. and Longitude, $13°$ and $20°$ W. from Washington. It is bounded on the N. by Minnesota, on the E. by Illinois, on the south by Missouri, and on the W. by Nebraska.

[Several hands raised.]

Teacher—Robert.

Robert—It is bounded on the W. by Dakota also.

Teacher—Very good. Any other criticisms or additions to what has been said on this point? [Mary's hand is raised.] What is it Mary?

Mary—It lies between the great rivers, the Mississippi and Missouri.

Teacher—Very good. That fact, however, will come out under the topic, Rivers. Katy you may tell us something about its size.

Katy—Its area is 55,045 square miles.

Teacher—That is correct, but you could not probably remember that number very long. Try and remember the round number, 55000. But let us compare it with other states and countries. [Hands raised.] George.

George—Georgia, Florida and Michigan are each a little larger. It is larger than either New York or Pennsylvania.

[Teacher calls on William whose hand is raised.]

William—It is very nearly the size of Illinois, and more than forty times as large as Rhode Island, the smallest state, and one-fifth as large as Texas, the largest state.

[Henry is called upon.] Henry—It is larger than either Ireland or Scotland and somewhere near the size of England.

NOTE.—In the following model recitations in this book it is understood that the teacher has called upon the pupil whose name precedes the answer. The pupils raise their hands when wishing to criticise or report additional matter and when a question is put to the class as a whole. The teacher selects the pupil whom he wishes shall answer the question and calls him by name. Snapping fingers to attract the teacher's attention should not be allowed. The most backward pupils should be most frequently called upon, the brighter ones will raise their hands the most frequently and get the benefit of the recitation without special effort on the part of the teacher.

Teacher—Carrie, describe the surface of Iowa.

Carrie—There are no mountains or very high hills. There are bluffs along the streams. It is called a Prairie State, but there is a considerable amount of timber on the banks of the streams. It has a general slope to the south.

Teacher—Anything further under this head?

John—There are two minor drainage slopes, one south-eastward to the Mississippi, the other south-westward to the Missouri.

Teacher—Class, how can you tell by looking at a map what direction the land slopes?

Mary—By the way the rivers run. They always run down hill.

Teacher—What is the ridge of land from which the water flows in opposite directions called?

Many voices—A water shed.

Teacher—James, what of the rivers of Iowa?

James—The Mississippi River forms its eastern boundary and the Missouri its western. The principal rivers in the interior of the State are the Des Moines, Skunk, Iowa and Cedar rivers which run towards the south-east and empty into the Mississippi. The Little Sioux and Nishnabotany run south-west and empty into the Missouri.

Teacher—Albert, what of Lakes?

Albert—There are no large lakes, but numerous small ones in the northern part. The largest is Spirit Lake containing about 12 square miles.

Henry—The Walled Lakes are great curiosities. There is an embankment of earth all around them as though thrown up by the hand of man.

Teacher—Can any one explain this phenomenon. [No answer.] I will leave this point until to-morrow. I want each one to try and find an explanation. Ask your parents or, perhaps, some of you have a large atlas of Iowa, which will explain it. There is a natural cause for this singular phenomenon and I want you to find it out. We will pass to the next topic.

This is sufficient to illustrate the manner of conducting a recitation in Advanced Geography. The teacher who can not get up enthusiasm in his class in this way is a failure. The remainder of the recitation will be similar to the foregoing. If the time will not permit the full discussion of one state, make two or more lessons of it. The map drawn by the pupil sent to the board should be criticised before the close of the recitation and the necessary talk about the next lesson should not be neglected. The teacher may impart some information not found in the text-books, concerning the next lesson, give instructions as to the manner of study, &c., &c. When the next recitation is called the first step should be a review of the last lesson and to call up any points left over for investigation.

PRIMARY GEOGRAPHY.

I here give a report of a lesson to a class just beginning the study. The teacher steps to the board and draws a straight line, saying, Children, we are now going to commence the study of Geography. The word means a description of the surface of the earth. We live on the earth and Geography describes what we may see on its surface or outside. We are going to begin right at home. Suppose I should want to write to one of my friends in Ohio and tell him that I was teaching school and wanted to describe to him just what kind of a school-room I had and how every thing was arranged in it, how could I best make it plain to him? Hands up now, all who can answer.

John. John—You could make a picture of the school-house and send it to him.

Teacher—Yes, that would show it plainly, but I can not draw well enough to make a picture and if I could it would take a good deal of time. Can you think of no other way? I will tell you. I can draw a map of this school-room, so that our friend in Ohio can see exactly how we are situated here. First, we must know something about direction. Who can tell me which direction I am pointing, (pointing to the north). Several voices—north. How do you know that is north. (No answer). Well, where does the sun rise? Mary.

Mary—In the east.

Teacher—And where does the sun set?

Mary—In the west.

Teacher—Very well, now if you stand with your right hand pointing to the east and your left hand pointing to the west, your face will be to the north and your back, where, class?

Several voices—To the south.

Teacher—Well, now you know the directions. On a map we always represent the top part as north and the bottom will be what, of course, then, class? *South.*

Teacher—And the right hand will be what? *East.* And the left? *West.* This line, I have drawn on the board will represent the north and this, (drawing another line parallel to it), the south, and these lines, (connecting the two) will represent east and west. Now we have shown the north, south, east and west sides of our school-room by straight lines. Now who will step to the board and make a dot to represent the right place for the stove? (A pupil steps up and makes a mark). Is that right, class? (Hands go up). John.

John—I think it should be nearer the south.

Teacher—Yes, (pupil changes it) now it is about right.

In this manner give each one of the class an opportunity to mark some point on the map.

Teacher—Now children, we have a map of the schoolroom. It is much easier made than a picture and it shows where everything is placed. We could draw a map of the school-house yard in the same way and tomorrow we will draw one. We could also draw the map of a man's farm, or of the school district which is made up of a number of farms, or of the township which is made up of a number of districts, and so on to the county and state. Here we have maps in our books of the states. These crooked lines represent rivers, or creeks, these dots, towns and cities. The states are colored differently so as to make them appear plainer on paper. We could not make a picture of any thing so large as a county or state. We can only draw a picture of what we can see with the eye by standing in one place. But by travelling we know that this is a very large earth on which we live. We can see only a small part at one time. Now no one man has travelled enough to see everything, but many different men have travelled, many different ones have written down what they have seen, and drawn maps of small portions and measured distances and so by putting all these together we get a complete description of the earth and are able to represent it on paper by lines and dots and colors, and these representations we call maps, and the descriptions of places and of things on the surface of the earth is called Geography. Now, how many think they can tell me to-morrow what Geography is and what a map is? (All hands go up). Very well, I will ask you to-morrow. But I must now give you something for to-morrow's lesson. I will write some words on the board and I want you to go to your books and find the words and find out what they mean. The books will tell you. You will find them on page (here shows them the place) and I want you all to be able to tell me what these words mean. These words are:

1. Continent.
2. Island.
3. Peninsula.
4. Cape.
5. Isthmus.

This will do for your lesson. Write these words on your slates as soon as you take your seats. If any do not understand what I mean, speak and I will explain further. Class excused.

U. S. HISTORY.

The first day the teacher has explained to the class his mode of teaching, and by reading with the class the first few pages of some school history, he has developed the following outline, and it is now on the blackboard.

Discovery of America.

1. Alleged Discovery by Northmen.
2. Circumstances which led to the Discovery by Columbus.
3. Nativity and Character of Columbus.
4. Difficulties in the way.
5. Ferdinand and Isabella.
6. The Voyage.
7. Land Discovered and Date.
8. Other Voyages of Columbus.
9. Death of Columbus.

Teacher—Henry, what can you tell us about the first discovery of America?

Henry—I could not find anything about the Northmen in my book. It commences with Columbus. (Hands*up).

Teacher—Philip. Philip—The Northmen claimed to have discovered this country about the year 1001.

Teacher—Who were the Northmen?

Philip—They were the people who lived in Norway, Sweden and Iceland.

Teacher—This question is not of great importance. It is very probable that these northern sea kings, as they were called, sailed westward and landed on the coast of North America, but they made no permanent settlements and the route was lost and the existence of this Continent forgotten. David, you may tell us what you can in regard to the second topic.

David—Men had come to believe that the earth was a sphere and supposed that Asia extended east until it nearly reached the western extremities of Europe. The mariner's compass had been invented and men were enabled to make voyages out of the sight of land. Men had a great desire to find a nearer route to Asia as India and China were celebrated for their great riches and trade had been carried on with them for many years.

Teacher—Very good, David. Has any one anything further on this point?

George—I read somewhere that pieces of carved wood and some strange plants had been washed on the shores of Portugal, which led Columbus to think there was land beyond the waters.

Joseph—And a canoe, and the bodies of two men different from the people of Europe were washed on shore.

Teacher—Yes, these are some of the principal circumstances which led Columbus to attempt this wonderful work. James, you may take the next topic.

James—Columbus was born in Genoa, Italy, in the year 1435. I can not tell anything about his character. I suppose he must have been a great man.

Teacher—Yes, Columbus was indeed a great man for he accomplished a great work, but what is necessary to make a man great? Suppose Columbus had said, "Well, I suppose there is a new route to the Indies to be discovered by sailing west and it would be a great thing to accomplish, but I have no means, I can do nothing;" do you think this Continent would have ever been discovered by him? It was energy and perseverance which made Columbus a great man. He was not disheartened by difficulties, but worked away until his object was accomplished. But this brings us to the next topic, The Difficulties in the Way. Charles, you may enlighten us upon this point.

Charles—Columbus was poor and had no means of his

own. He applied to his own government and then to the King of Portugal and then to Spain but was met with a refusal each time.

I will not carry this any further. The reader has some idea now of the manner of conducting a recitation. It is not to be supposed, of course, that the pupils will all answer so well as here represented, and it must be held in mind that much is omitted. The remarks made by the teacher and the questions asked to draw out backward pupils, if all given here would occupy too much space. When the teacher has thus gone through with the topic outline he should recapitulate the main points in concert or otherwise, and write on the blackboard the principal date or dates. In this lesson there should be but one date put down, 1492.

Encourage pupils to tell what they know in their own language. You can always tell when they are quoting the language of the text-book. It is far better that they use their own language, though it be ungrammatical, hesitating and crude. You have the opportunity then to criticise and correct their language and thus incidentally cultivate their powers of expression.

The story of Columbus is a most interesting one. It is much more important that the class spend considerable time getting the interesting details of this subject in order to fix the main facts and date, than to commit to memory the names and dates of all the discoverers and explorers from that time down to the settlement at Jamestown. Several lessons may be made on the outline above, giving different pupils different topics each time to report upon. The next lesson to be outlined may be, *Other Discoveries.* Under this may be brought out the principal voyages and discoveries only, and will bring the subject down to the period of settlement. The pupils should write these topics on their slates, or it would be well to have them write on paper, or in a blank book and preserve them for future use.

The energetic teacher will gather from these few hints the true method of teaching history.

GRAMMAR.

The outline on page — being on the board the teacher and class discuss it somewhat as follows:

Teacher—Mary, can you tell me what a noun is?

Mary—A noun is a name.

Teacher—Yes. Every noun is a name, and every name is a noun. All those words which are the names of objects which you can see, hear, feel, taste or smell, and all words which are names of qualities of objects, as goodness, sweetness, all names of anything you can conceive of, as peace, purity, love, joy, &c. Mary, what noun in this sentence? Riches take to themselves wings and fly away.

Mary—Riches.

Teacher—Why?

Mary—Because it is the name of something.

Teacher—Now we have different kinds of nouns and I have here arranged the different kinds in an outline that I may better fix them in your minds. I have made two classes, General and Special, that is all nouns are either Common or Proper, but then we sometimes have them arranged in special classes as Abstract, Verbal, Collective and Class nouns. You have studied your lesson in the book as I wished you, to and now who can tell me what a Common noun is? Carrie.

Carrie—A Common noun is a common name or a name common to a class of objects, as book, tree, house, etc.

Teacher—Yes. When we say book, we do not mean any particular book but the name applies to books as a class of objects. Class, is horse a common noun? Yes. Why? Because it is a name common to a class of animals.

The teacher will multiply such examples as these, as he thinks necessary.

Teacher—James, what is a Proper noun?

James—A proper noun is the name of a particular individual or object as John, New York, etc.

Teacher—Yes. When I say John, I do not mean any boy or man, but one particular boy or man whose name is John, so when I say New York I do not mean any city but that particular city which is named New York. I think you now understand the distinctions of Common and Proper nouns. But here is a point I wish you to bear in mind, that Proper nouns are always written with a capital letter and never in any other way. If you see the name of a town or person spelled without a capital, anywhere, you may know it is a mistake, it makes no difference who wrote it. I want you to remember this. Thousands of people make such mistakes every day. Never make this mistake. If you learn nothing else here to-day, remember this, and if you put it into practice always, it may be worth hundreds of dollars to you. You seem surprised, but let me explain. Suppose I had charge of a large school where there were several teachers employed and I wanted to hire a man to teach in my school. Suppose I should get a letter from a man making application for a school and he should address the envelope in the way, I here write it on the board: *danville, indiana*. Do you suppose I would read the letter any further? He may be an intelligent man and a good teacher in many respects, but I would not think so from the letter, and I would not waste further time trying to find out. In ninety-nine cases out of a hundred I would save time by not even opening his letter. So in all kinds of business such little matters as these go a great way. Let me urge you to take particular pains to spell and capitalize properly, if you do not make such great advances in other things. There are other rules for the use of capitals, but this is one of great importance and I wish to impress it on your minds.

In a similar manner let the remainder of the outline be discussed. The teacher need not talk so much as here represented, but the pupil should be encouraged to criticise, ask questions, and give definitions. I have here given a rather lengthy talk for the teacher in order to illustrate the manner in which it is necessary, sometimes, to talk to a class.

ADVANCED ARITHMETIC.

The class are using *Ray's Third Part*. Each pupil is going as fast as he can. It is impossible to keep a class together in a country school, owing to irregularity of attendance. The pupils are working in various parts of Profit and Loss.

Teacher—On page 248, the 8th example, Charles; the

7th, James. On page 249, the 7th, Mary; the 8th, William; the 9th, Lucy. On page 250, Henry, the 10th. Place your examples on the board as rapidly as possible. Let us see how neat you can make your work.

While this section is at the black-board the teacher gives the remainder of the class to whom he has not assigned examples, an oral drill, asking questions on the principles involved and making inquiries of each pupil as to progress, or explaining some point left over from last lesson.

By this time James is ready to explain his example.

James—Example 8, p. 248. "A bought 40 bales of cotton, at $40 each, and sold it at a profit of $704; what per cent. did he make?"

Operation:

$$\begin{array}{c}\$40\\40\\\hline\$1600\end{array}\quad \frac{704}{1600}=\frac{176}{400}=\frac{44}{100}=.44=44 \text{ per cent.}$$

Explanation: If one bale of cotton cost $40, 40 bales will cost 40 times $40 which are $1600. He sold it for $704 more than it cost him. $704 is $\frac{704}{1600}$ of 1600, therefore he gained $\frac{704}{1600}$ of what it cost. $\frac{704}{1600}=\frac{44}{100}=44$ per cent.

Teacher—What other way could this have been solved, class?

Henry—Divide $704 by $1600 and express the quotient in decimal hundredths.

Teacher—The principle is just the same, but James' method is much plainer. He has given an analysis of the example. Very good, James, you are excused. Lucy may explain next.

Lucy—Example 9th, p. 249. " By selling tea at $1.19 per pound, I lost 15 per cent; what the cost price per ℔?

Operation:

```
 1.00   .85 | 1.1900 | 1.40
  .15         85
  ___         ___
  .85         340
              340
              ___
               0
```

Explanation: 15 per cent. is 15 cents on the dollar, so what cost me $1.00 if I lose 15 cts., I must sell for $1.00—$.15 which is $.85, so as often as $.85 is contained in the selling price $1.19, so many times is $1.00 contained in the cost price. $1.19÷.85=1.40=$1.40.

When mistakes are made either in the expression on the board or in the explanation, the teacher should call out criticisms from the class and make such comments himself as he may deem necessary.

Teacher—Observe, class, that the per cent. of gain or loss is always estimated on the cost and never on the selling price. This is a very simple principle if you will just think that you can not tell whether you are going to gain or lose on any article which you are going to sell unless you know what it cost you. If you sell for less than cost, you lose; if for more than cost, you gain. Although it is very simple, here is just where a great many fail in solving these examples.

REMARKS.

I have in this chapter given a few model lessons, or partial lessons, sufficient, I think, to illustrate the manner of teaching these branches. It is not necessary to give a model lesson in each branch as the idea may be easily grasped from these here given when taken in connection with the chapters on the respective branches. It would be impossible to represent on paper the actual work of a recitation conducted by a live teacher, but it is hoped these few examples will prove suggestive and awaken the true method in the teacher who begins as a tyro in the work.

CHAPTER XII.

MISCELLANEOUS.

Under this head I propose to make a few suggestions which could not well be classified under any of the foregoing chapters. I shall not have any general order or plan, but shall, in a discursive, irregular way, offer some thoughts not spoken of before in this book, and perhaps recapitulate and add something to what has already been said.

1. *Unconscious Teaching.* In the opening chapter I have hinted at the fact that a man teaches when he least seems to be teaching. All that a man does and thinks goes to make up his character, and a man's character impresses itself upon all who come in contact with him. If his life has been filled with good deeds and thoughts, a certain good influence will flow from him and exert itself upon all with whom he deals, even upon those who know nothing of his former life. On the contrary, if he has been a bad man, has committed crimes, or indulged to a great extent in wicked thoughts, a bad influence will emanate from him, and influence all upon whom it falls.

We are all, to a certain extent, character readers. We read persons by their manner, by their conversation, by their looks. Small children, even, are good readers of character, although they could not tell you by what rules they judge. We take a liking or disliking to persons, and we cannot tell why.

> " I do not love you, Dr. Fell,
> The reason why I can not tell;
> But this alone I know full well,
> I do not love you, Dr. Fell."

But this much is true, that a good man will be generally liked by everybody, that is, they will like him personally, though they may hate his actions, or his principles, because not in accordance with their own notions; and a hypocrite will be generally despised however well he may play his part.

Every thought and action of your life from infancy to manhood, has a bearing more or less direct on your work as a teacher. In other words, the teacher commences to develop in influence and constantly adds to his character that which will make him either a good teacher, or an inferior one.

Remember, then, teacher, that you are always teaching when in contact with others. The teacher should be in every sense a man. Strive to cultivate that true manhood. Keep a watch upon your thoughts and actions, and daily and hourly build a character that will constantly teach the good, and the good only.

But there are some men that are not very good nor very bad, sort of wooden men, mere automatons or puppets, who can tell what they have learned, as a parrot says its phrase or an inferior stage actor his piece. You often find them in the school-room. Such men have so little character that they do very little unconscious teaching. Their presence teaches but little, because they have so little character to exert an influence. For all the good their presence does, the knowledge might as well be sent into the school-room through a telephone.

Again there are men whose very looks and manners teach lessons. You feel their magnetic force when you take them by the hand, and gather inspiration from their eyes. The successful teacher, as well as the men who move the world, belong to this class.

2. *Have Sympathy for Pupils.* The true method of teaching is drawn from Nature. If we observe how a child acquires new ideas when left to itself, we may learn how to teach it. When a child makes a new discovery, or gets a new idea, the first thing it does is to make some one else acquainted with the fact. How eager the child is to show its mother any new object it finds, or to tell about any novelty it has seen. Observe how a boy will act after he has been to a circus show. Even the infant will hold up its toys for you to look at and admire. We should infer from this, that children need encouragement in all their studies by a kind of attentive sympathy with all their eoflrts to acquire knowledge. When a child has drawn a picture, or formed a letter on the slate, and holds it up for you to look at, you ignore one of the first principles of teaching if you fail to notice the child's effort. This principle should be carried out with all grades of pupils. Take special pains to notice their efforts and give kind words of encouragement. Never make discouraging remarks about a pupil's work. If they have through carelessness failed to

do as well as you think they are capable of doing, never make sport of their work nor scold, but say, "that does pretty well, but I think you can do better if you try." Always make favorable comments whenever you can conscientiously, but never compare one pupil's work with another's. In the work of the best pupils you can point out some defects, and in the work of the poorest pupils, you may find something upon which you can favorably comment. By thus taking an interest in, and showing a sympathy for their efforts you will encourage greater effort and secure the good will of all your pupils.

3. *Ride no Hobbies.* The true teacher has no pet theory nor patent method of teaching. He is ready at any time to abandon a plan as soon as he finds something better. He is always open to conviction. He is progressive, and aggressive, radical and even fanatical in the search for truth, yet conservative and cautious about adopting new methods until he has given them thorough study. He has a variety of plans and uses, different plans for different circumstances. He will not try to make a square block fill a round hole. He will find objections to all methods and adopt that which, after mature deliberation, he finds to be the least objectionable.

4. *Study Your own Failures.* "The burnt child dreads the fire." Here again we have Nature's method of teaching. He makes greatest advances who is able to see his own mistakes. He who is bigoted and self-conceited and never sees his own errors, will make but little progress in anything he undertakes. The teacher should observe closely the results of his plans and note

where they are successful, and where a failure, and should govern his future accordingly. Let him review each evening the work of the day and try and find a mistake he has made, and resolve to do better the next day. A man should criticise himself severely, sparing no self-scrutiny with regard to his own actions.

5. *Make the School-Room Attractive.* The teacher can do something towards relieving the monotony of bare walls and plain desks and uncarpeted floor. In the first place, he should keep the school-room clean, and in order; and next by use of pictures, mottoes, wreaths and flowers make it as attractive a place as possible. The school-room should be as attractive in appearance as the average homes of the pupils. The nature of our daily surroundings has much to do in forming our characters. I might enlarge upon this point, but will not occupy the space, as the fact will be granted by the intelligent reader. You need not go to any considerable expense. Get a few pictures framed and purchase a half-dozen mottoes, and keep them as a part of your stock in trade. Your pictures may be chromos, lithographs, or steel engravings which will not cost much when neatly framed, but will, if selected with taste, form very attractive adornments for the walls. Let the subjects be animals, flowers, landscapes, or portraits of distinguished men. Anything in the style appropriate to a bar-room or saloon will, of course, be out of place in the school-room. If framed pictures can not be procured, the engravings from illustrated papers pasted on the walls with wreaths of evergreens encircling them, will form very attractive objects, for a time at least. A card motto surrounded with a wreath of

evergreens, makes a very neat appearance on the wall. Winter boquets may be made of everlasting flowers, ornamental grasses, &c. If the school-room can be kept warm enough, a few house plants might be kept through the winter, and will add much to the cheerfulness of the place. During Spring and Fall terms, plants and flowers can be had in abundance, and they should form a part of the school-room decorations.

I need not suggest any further to the teacher who has a love for the beautiful. If you love the school-room and school work, and are a true man or woman, you will profit by these suggestions.

6. *The Teacher's Library.* Books are to the teacher what tools are to the mechanic. As a mechanic can get along with a limited number of tools, so a teacher can get along with a limited number of books, but as certain tools are essential to a mechanic, so certain books are essential to the teacher. I would not advise the young teacher to spend a great part of his earnings for books, nor to go in debt for them, but there are a few books which he ought to have, at almost any sacrifice, if he would be a good teacher. Let him go without paper collars, without tea or coffee, without anything finer than jeans pants, rather than without an Unabridged Dictionary. Let him board himself and live on ten cents a day rather than do without certain necessary books. I do not hesitate to say that any teacher can so economize his means, can by cutting off an expense here and denying himself there, save money enough during one or two terms of school to procure the essentials of a teacher's library.

An Unabridged Dictionary (Webster's is more generally recognized, although Worcester's is also a standard) is an indispensable part of a teacher's outfit. The Unabridged is a whole library in itself. There are few subjects upon which valuable information can not be had by consulting its pages. There are many men who own Dictionaries who know but little of what they contain. I would not only advise the purchase of an Unabridged, but insist on its constant use. If you are not already pretty thoroughly read, you will find use for the Dictionary in reading almost any species of composition you may take up. You should look up the meaning of every word about which you have the slightest doubt.

You should look up the meaning of many simple words, the Anglo-Saxon monosyllables which you have used from infancy, words which you hear in daily conversation, and meet with in your daily reading. You will find the Dictionary valuable reading, notwithstanding, as the old lady said, the subject changes frequently. Study the etymology of words. It will help you greatly in retaining their meaning in your memory.

There are many books designed to help teachers, but from which the country teacher can obtain but little practical knowledge. I can call to mind about twenty different works on teaching and school management, which I have read or examined, and among the number I could recommend but two or three which would be of great benefit to a country teacher. Of course, there is much in them that is valuable, but scattered through so much that is merely theoretical and impracticable that it would not pay the outlay. I would advise, of course, that you purchase works on education and read them, but beware of buying too many books at one time. It would be a good rule never to buy a new book until you have read the last one thoroughly. There is one book, however, I must recommend to every teacher. Though old and though written for students, yet as the truth it contains will never grow old, and as the teacher should be always a student, I can recommend it as next in importance to the Unabridged Dictionary. It is the Student's Manual, by Rev. John Todd, D. D., a work, though small, containing more sensible advice than any work I can call to mind.

One text-book, at least, on each of the following sciences will gradually find its way into your library. Physics, Chemistry, Botany, Zoology, Physiology, and Geology. The ordinary text-books designed for schools, will answer your purpose at first. If you have a class in Physiology it will be of advantage to you to procure some larger treatise than the ordinary text-book. A good work on Composition and Rhetoric will be valuable. A history of the U. S. larger than those designed for schools, and an outline of universal history, will be valuable aids in teaching this branch and for self-improvement.

There are four books I would like to name here which the teacher may procure when he gets able, and which he will find valuable as bearing more or less directly upon his profession. I will name them in the order in which he should obtain and read them. Herbert Spencer's Essay on Education; Deterioration and Race Education, Royce; Educational Reformers, Quick; Scientific Basis of Education, Hecker. These four volumes will give him a pretty thorough knowledge of the science of education, and they are standard and valuable works, deserving a place in every scholar's library, whatever profession he may follow. They are to be studied, not merely read and laid aside.

If the teacher wishes to dip into science, he will find a mine of treasures in the International Series of Scientific books, published by D. Appleton & Co., New York. I would advise the teacher to procure the catalogues of the leading publishing houses and read the notices of new books, which are continually appearing. By keeping posted as to what the world of authors is doing, you will be able to select good books only, and buying them as you are able, you will, in time, build up a library of great value to you in whatever profession you may finally choose.

I would just say here that there are several books annually published by the U. S. government, and designed for the improvement of those who are interested in the respective subjects. Among those I would recommend to teachers, are the Reports of the Smithsonian Institute, to be obtained of the Secretary of the Institution; the Reports of the Commissioner of Education, to be obtained of the Commissioner of Education. If these parties are addressed at Washington, D. C., by letter, stating plainly the book wanted and the year issued, they will be sent gratis. These works are frequently distributed by members of Congress to particular friends, often for political purposes, and thus do not reach the parties who would make good use of them. The teacher needs these works, and the government designs that such parties should have them. It should be remembered that they are always issued a year or more after the year for which they are the report. For example, the report for 1877 will be had sometime during the first of the year 1879, or latter part of 1878.

By economy, by abstaining from habits such as chewing and smoking, any young man, can, in a few years, save enough to procure a good library. If all the money which is spent by young men from the time they are sixteen years of age until they are twenty-five to gratify their appetites and morbid tastes, was saved and invested in good books, they would have a library, of which any man of intellectual taste might well be proud. Never say, then, that you are too poor to buy books so long as you indulge in expensive habits.

A good book is a treasure and does not even get old. Says Milton, "A good book is the precious life-blood of a master spirit, embalmed and treasured up for a life to come." Commence then, young teacher, to build a library. Commence with one book and add to it as your means will allow, and you will, in a few years, be surprised at the result, and if you make judicious selections and good use of your books, you will also have a library in your head.

Borrow all the books you can if they are such as you think will profit you to read. If you take good care of books, and are prompt to return them, you can always borrow.

7. *Exercise Your Pen.* Lord Bacon said, "Reading maketh a full man, writing an exact man." If you would profit by what you read and think, write your thoughts down. It is a good habit always to read with a pen or pencil in hand. Many an idea is lost because not written down. The mind receives ideas one after

another and cannot retain them all, although each makes its impression. They will make a double impression by the act of writing them, and at the same time be preserved for future rehearsal when the mind has forgotten the form in which they came, besides, by writing you are improving yourself in the power of expression, you are cultivating language. Take notes of your reading and write down any ideas which your reading may suggest.

Write essays on easy subjects, even though no one else ever sees them. Your first efforts will be of little benefit to any one but yourself, but they will be of great benefit to you. Lay them aside for a year and then take them up and read them critically. You will find many errors, and see where you could make great improvements. Be the local reporter of yonr neighborhood. Write for your county paper. Local editors are always anxious to have a correspondent in each village or township. The teacher is eminently fitted to fill that position, and the exercise will be of great benefit to him. By thus commencing on a small scale, you will, by and by, be able to write for educational journals, for magazines, &c. I advise you thus to exercise your pen continually for your own improvement, and when you have improved yourself to a certain extent, your pen will enlighten others, and thus you will become an educator as well as a learner. Who knows what future Greeleys may come from among the country school teachers.

8. *Recipe for Blackboard.* The teacher may find school-rooms as I have found them, without sufficient blackboard. A good blackboard may be made for about fifty cents–not more than that. I cannot tell where

this recipe came from, but I have used it in several schoolhouses.

Take equal parts of lamp black and flower of emory, and thin with a mixture of equal parts of benzine and Japan varnish. Apply two coats to any smooth plastered wall.

Where boards of education will not furnish plenty of blackboard the teacher may make them ashamed of themselves for half a dollar.

9. *Teaching Penmanship.* I have ommitted saying anything about teaching penmanship in former chapters. A word about it here will not be out of place. The writing lesson should come near the close of the day, and not immediately after play hour, for the reason that pupils are tired of study, and writing is a kind of rest from more active mental work, and after pupils have been at their seats awhile their muscles and nerves have become quieted.

If the teacher has not charts to illustrate the principles of Penmanship, he should procure a colored crayon, and draw on the plastered wall a diagram illustrating all the principles, and a copy of all the letters made according to system just as they are in the charts or copper-plate copy-books. He should insist on all the pupils having Spencerian copy-books, or some other similar kind. The practice of writing copies should no longer hold. The teacher will, however, be obliged to fight against the combined opposition of parents and pupils in some districts.

The forms and principles of the letters should be studied. The pupil should not be allowed simply to copy the letter, but should study it until he has an ideal of it in his mind, and then with his eyes fixed upon his pen, attempt to reproduce the ideal on paper. The old way was to fix one eye on the pen and the other on the copy, and try to imitate it, or if such an ocular feat was impossible, the eyes were alternately fixed on the copy and on the pen. When a letter is formed by the pupil, it should be compared with the copy and the defects pointed out. As a drill for the class, the teacher may make certain letters on the black-board, showing the different faults of the pupils, and ask them to point out the faults. Many other exercises will readily suggest themselves to the thinking teacher.

Pens, ink, and copy-books should never be allowed to remain in the pupils' desks. They should be collected at the close of the writing exercise, and distributed again when needed. Pupils should be encouraged to take a pride in keeping their copy-books clean and neat.

10. *The Teacher's Highest Reward.* The compensation paid teachers for their services is small in comparison with the rewards of those who follow other professions. The wages of the best paid teachers are extremely low compared with the income of a first-class lawyer or physician. Some preachers also get large salaries. But professional men generally do not make fortunes. The great fortunes are nearly always made by merchants, or what are called business men. If your highest aim, young man, is to get rich, to amass a colossal fortune, do not enter a profession. But professional men see pleasure in the pursuit of something beside wealth. The highest pleasures flow from the action of the intellect. An Agassiz, who said he had no time to

make money enjoyed existence, I venture to assert, much more than a Vanderbilt or an Astor.

The teacher who finds not pleasure in the pursuit of his profession, or in the action of his intellect, would better quit the profession at once, and engage in some other pursuit. But there are times when the best of teachers feel discouraged. There are times when their labors seem in vain. They have labored patiently day in and day out, and their work seems like the labors of Sisyphus, who was doomed to roll a stone to the top of a hill, and in spite of all his efforts it continually returned upon him. But remember, teacher, that your work is sometimes like bread cast upon the waters, to bear fruit after many days. When such thoughts come over you read the following poem which is such an excellent piece of composition, and so aptly hits the point, that I cannot refrain from quoting it entire. It is from the pen of W. H. Venable, author of a school history of the United States, and other educational works, distinguished alike as an educator, author, and poet:

THE TEACHER'S DREAM.

The weary teacher sat alone
 While twilight gathered on;
And not a sound was heard around,
 The boys and girls were gone.

The weary teacher sat alone,
 Unnerved and pale was he;
Bowed 'neath a yoke of care, he spoke
 In sad soliloquy:

"Another round, another round
 Of labor thrown away,—
Another chain of toil and pain
 Dragged through a tedious day.

"Of no avail is constant zeal,
  Love's sacrifice is loss,
The hopes of morn, so golden, turn,
  Each evening, into dross.

"I squander on a barren field,
  My strength, my life, my all;
The seeds I sow will never grow,
  They perish where they fall."

He sighed, and low upon his hands
  His aching brow he prest;
And o'er his frame, erelong there came
  A soothing sense of rest.

And then he lifted up his face,
  But started back aghast,—
The room by strange and sudden change
  Assumed proportions vast.

It seemed a Senate hall, and one
  Addressed a listening throng;
Each burning word all bosoms stirred,
  Applause rose loud and long.

The 'wildered teacher thought he knew
  The speaker's voice and look,
"And for his name," said he, "the same
  Is in my record book."

The stately Senate hall dissolved,
  A church rose in its place,
Wherein there stood a man of God,
  Dispensing words of grace.

And though he spoke in solemn tone,
  And though his hair was gray,
The teacher's thought was strangely wrought:
  "I whipped that boy to-day."

The church, a phantasm, vanished soon;
  What saw the teacher then?
In classic gloom of alcoved room,
  An author plied his pen.

>   My idlest lad!" the teacher said,
>   Filled with new surprise—
>   "Shall I behold *his* name enrolled
>   Among the great and wise?"
>
>   The vision of a cottage home
>   The teacher now descried;
>   A mother's face illumed the place
>   Her influence sanctified.
>
>   "A miracle! a miracle!
>   This matron, well I know,
>   Was but a wild and careless child,
>   Not half an hour ago.
>
>   'And when she to her children speaks
>   Of duty's golden rule,
>   Her lips repeat, in accents sweet,
>   My words to her at school."
>
>   The scene was changed again, and lo,
>   The school-house rude and old,
>   Upon the wall did darkness fall,
>   The evening air was cold.
>
>   "A dream!" the sleeper, waking, said,
>   Then paced along the floor,
>   And, whistling slow and soft and low,
>   He locked the school-house door.
>
>   And walking home, his heart was full
>   Of peace and trust and love and praise;
>   And singing slow and soft and low,
>   He murmured, "After many days."

There are many other things I might suggest to the teacher, but as they are so admirably illustrated in the little book already mentioned, viz: Todd's Student's Manual, I will advise the teacher to procure a copy at once rather than I should iterate what has been so much better said. There is one matter, however, which I hope to be pardoned for mentioning as a closing piece of advice to the teacher. It is a delicate matter and I wish to handle it carefully. Let me whisper it in your ear. If you are not already mated for life, and have a home which is dearer to you than all else beside, I advise you to seek out a congenial spirit, who will share your joys and sympathize with you in your difficulties, and be in all things a helpmeet and adviser through life. I hope to see the day in this country, when the country school-house shall have within a stone's throw, a cottage and an acre or two of ground to be let to the teacher who will make it his home, where he can cultivate the soil for his partial sustenance, and where he can have the needful exercise for his muscles, and an opportunity to gratify his taste in growing flowers and fruits. I might grow poetical here, but there is no need of it. This is intended as a practical work and I will leave others the task of furnishing the dessert of the teacher's table. I have only attempted to furnish some wholesome bread and meat for the tyro teacher, and how well I have executed my task, I leave the reader to judge.

CHAPTER XIII.

HINTS AND HELPS FOR THE TEACHER.

Gen. Sheridan wrote to Gen. Grant, "Things are in a shape to push." Grant replied, "Push things." Let me say to you, teacher, *country* teacher though you are, *Push things.* Though you may have the dingiest log school-house, among the rudest of back-woods-men, for your theater of operations, let me repeat to you, *Push things.* If things are not in a shape to push, put them in a shape to push, and then PUSH. You must have push, vim, energy, call it what you will, *you must have that which will make things go* if you would succeed.

Read the following extracts from some of the leading thinkers and educators of the world. You may gather inspiration from them and be prompted to take renewed interest in your work:

Ideas make their way in silence like the waters that, filtering behind the rocks of the Alps, loosen them from the mountains on which they rest.—*D'Aubigne.*

In the end thought rules the world. There are times when impulses and passions are more powerful, but they soon expend themselves; while *mind*, acting constantly, is ever ready to drive them back and work when their energy is exhausted.—*McCosh.*

I do not think that it is the mission of this age, or of any other age, to lay down a system of education which shall hold good for all ages. Let us never forget that the present century has just as good a right to its forms of thought and methods of culture as any former centuries had to theirs, and that the same resources of power are open to us to-day as were ever open to humanity in any age of the world.—*Tyndall.*

The profession of the teacher can not be too highly estimated. It demands, for its highest success and usefulness, a special knowledge and training beyond the scope of the common learning and methodical discipline which it labors to impart. The teacher should know the Human Mind, and the bodily conditions upon which Mind depends.—*Hecker.*

People do not understand childhood. With the false notions we have of it the further we go the more we blunder. The wisest apply themselves to what it is important to *men* to know, without considering what *children* are in a condition to learn. They are always seeking the man in the *child*, without reflecting what he is before he can be a man. This is the study to which I have applied myself most; so that, should my practical scheme be found useless and chimerical, my observation will always turn to account. I may possibly have taken a very bad view of what ought to be done, but I conceive I have taken a good one of the subject to be wrought upon. Begin, then, by studying your pupils better; for most assuredly you do not at present understand them.—*Rousseau.*

The object of education, is to promote the normal growth of a human being, developing all his powers systematically and symmetrically, so as to give the greatest possible capability in thought and action.—*Prof. James Johonnot.*

Education must put the child to work; for by work man is perfected. And what he does not achieve, he never comprehends; and, hence, the barrenness of the word learning of the schools. It profits but little the individual, and none at all the race or nation.—*Samuel Royce.*

I discard as selfish in the extreme, that narrow principle, which would look down upon any branch of human knowledge as useless or improper, however widely they may differ in relative value. Some topics of study seem to have no object but the occupation and exercise, whether salutary or not, of the mental faculties; while others do not assert a principle, or move a step without contributing to the welfare and improvement of the human family.—*E. D. Mansfield.*

The school-master is one of the chief workmen, I may almost say the principal in preparing for the genius of America, in the bright years of that futurity, the most magnificent edifice that the mind of a nation ever inhabited.—*Thomas Smith Grimke.*

The greatest thing a human soul ever does in this world is to see something, and tell what it saw in a plain way. Hundreds of people can talk for one who can think, but thousands can think for one who can see.

To see clearly, is poetry, prophecy and religion, all in one.—*Ruskin.*

Man's actions here are of infinite moment to him, and never die or end at all. Man, with his little life, reaches upward high as heaven—downward low as hell; and in his three-score-years of time holds an eternity fearfully and wonderfully hidden.—*Thomas Carlyle.*

Oh, how hard it is to die, and not be able to leave the world any better for one's little life in it!—*Abraham Lincoln.*

The great secret of success in life is for a man to be ready when his opportunity comes.—*Disraeli.*

There is no credit in knowing how to spell, but positive disgrace in being ignorant on that point. So there can be no credit in doing right, while it is infamous to do wrong.—*George Francis Train.*

Censure and criticism never hurt anybody. If false, they can't hurt you unless you are wanting in manly character; and if true, they show a man his weak points and forewarn him against failure and trouble.—*Gladstone.*

The child, through stumbling, learns to walk erect. Every fall is upward.—*Theodore Parker.*

Old truths are always new to us if they come with the smell of heaven upon them.—*John Bunyan.*

Be a bold, brave, true, honest man. If you know a thing is right, do it. If you have a solemn conviction, dare to utter it in the fear of God, regardless of the wrath of man.—*John B. Gough.*

There is no temptation so great as not to be tempted at all.—*Hannah More.*

It is a principle of war, that when you can use the

thunder-bolt you must prefer it to the cannon. Earnestness is the thunder-bolt.—*Napoleon.*

If I take care of my character my reputation will take care of itself.—*Moody.*

I would rather be right than be President.—*Henry Clay.*

An instructed democracy is the surest foundation of Government, and education and freedom are the only sources of true greatness and true happiness among any people.—*John Bright.*

The doorstep to the temple of wisdom is a knowledge of our own ignorance.—*Spurgeon.*

Let the soldier be abroad if he will, he can do nothing in this age. There is another personage, a personage less imposing in the eyes of some, perhaps insignificant. The school-master is abroad, and I trust to him, armed with his primer against the soldier in full military array.—*Lord Brougham.*

Let every man be occupied, and occupied in the highest employment of which his nature is capable, and die with the consciousness that he has done his best.—*Sidney Smith.*

But under whose care soever a child is put to be taught, during the tender and flexible years of his life, this is certain, it should be one who thinks Latin and language the least part of education; one, who knowing how much virtue, and a well tempered soul, is to be preferred to any sort of learning or language, makes it his chief business to form the mind of his scholars, and give that a right disposition: which, if once got, though all the rest should be neglected, would, in due time, produce all the rest; and which if it be not got, and settled, so as to keep out ill and vicious habits, languages and sciences, and all other accomplishments of education, will be to no purpose, but to make the worse a more dangerous man.—*John Locke.—1690.*

In our country and in our times, no man is worthy the honored name of a statesman who does not include the highest practicable education of the people in all his plans of administration.—*Horace Mann.*

The teacher should permit his pupil himself to taste and relish things, and of himself to choose and discern them, sometimes opening the way to him, and sometimes making him break the ice himself; that is, I would not have the teacher alone to invent and speak, but that he should also hear his pupils speak. Socrates, and since him Arcesilaus, made first their scholars speak, and then spoke to them.—*Montaigne.—Written in the age of Queen Elizabeth.*

There is a most remarkable reciprocal action between the interest which the teacher takes and that which he communicates to his pupils. If he is not with his whole mind present at the subject, if he does not care whether he is understood or not, whether his manner is liked or not, he will alienate the affections of his pupils, and render them indifferent to what he says. But real interest taken in the task of instruction—kind words and kinder feelings—the very expression of the features, and the glance of the eye, are never lost upon children.—*Pestalozzi.*

Intelligence and virtue are the foundation and the corner stone of the American Republic. Hence, it follows that ignorance and wrong are its most formidable foes. Its theory is that every citizen must be intelligent enough clearly to comprehend, and virtuous enough faithfully to discharge his duties.—*Prof. Wm. F. Phelps.*

All who consider the subject must admit that the teacher is called to labor in a field of vast influence. This the teacher should understand, and, though he may at times feel almost crushed by the weight of his responsibilities, and be induced to exclaim, "Who is sufficient for these things?" yet let him persevere, trusting in Him from whom cometh all needed assistance, ever aiming at a nearer approximation to the mark of perfection, ever striving to remove defects and cultivate excellences.—*Northend.*

In the name of the living God it must be proclaimed, that licentiousness shall be the liberty—violence and chicanery shall be the law—superstition and craft shall be the religion—and the self-destructive indulgence of all sensual and unhallowed passions, shall be the only happiness of that people who neglect the education of their children.—*Hon. Newton Bateman.*

To teach, whether by word or action, is the greatest function on earth.—*Channing.*

We want men of original perception and original action, who can open their eyes wider than to a nationality, —namely, to considerations of benefit to the human race,—can act in the interest of civilization; men of classic, men of moral mind, who can live in the moment and take a step forward. Columbus was no backward creeping crab, nor was Martin Luther, nor John Adams, nor Patrick Henry, nor Thomas Jefferson; and the Genius or Destiny of America is no log or sluggard, but a man incessantly advancing, as the shadow on the dial's face, or the heavenly body by whose light it is marked.—*Ralph Waldo Emerson.*

Some teachers have learned how to read mind, to understand a class of pupils in a single day's observation. Some have learned how to encourage one and guide another, how to control each one according to his peculiarities. The teacher who knows this, as the musician knows how to bring out harmonies from the instrument, is the one who can teach easily and successfully, and proves to be the true teacher. Teachers should learn, then, how to read character, how to read the dispositions of each pupil, and how, therefore, to manipulate each one in the best manner to secure the highest success.—*Nelson Sizer.*

If we work upon marble, it will perish. If we work upon brass, time will efface it. If we rear temples, they will crumble into dust. But if we work upon immortal minds—if we imbue them with high principles—with the just fear of God and of their fellow men,—we engrave upon those tablets something which no time can efface, but which will brighten to all eternity.—*Daniel Webster.*

It requires more care and attention, more experience and sagacity, and a more intimate acquaintance with the principles of human nature, to direct the opening intellect *in its first excursions* in the path of knowledge, than to impart to it instructions respecting any particular science in after life.—*Thomas Dick.*

Before the earnestness of truth and sincerity, the glittering charms of wordy eloquence, or the seductive imagery of unhallowed genius, sink into insignificance. —*Mrs. Lincoln Phelps.*

The end of education is the power or art of *thinking*. This power is acquired, but never inborn. It is always the price of long-continued and patient study. Talents though "angel bright," and even genius, need culture, to be educated, as really as the most ordinary intellects. The mere absorption of knowledge, as the sponge absorbs water, gives no discipline; and hence the acquiring of knowledge is not the object to be gained, but the development of mental power.—*Orcutt.*

A believer in the doctrine "the physician born not made," (a motto on a par with "the teacher born, not made)," once said to a distinguished oculist, who was advocating the necessity of thorough training in his profession: "Why, doctor, you have attained the highest skill without such aid." The oculist replied, "But I spoiled a bushel of eyes in acquiring the art, and now I can teach others to avoid my blunders." Contrasts most marked I often witness in schools similar in other conditions, except that an expert teaches the one, and a novice experiments in the other. In the one you see order, interest, activity, cheerfulness, and joy of conscious progress; in the other, confusion, whispering and mischief, or listlessness, indolence, and dislike of study. —*B. G. Northrop.*

Wisdom is the principal thing; therefore get wisdom; and with all thy getting get understanding.—*Solomon.*

Education is intended to enlighten the intellect, to train it and the moral sentiments to vigor, and to repress the too great activity of the selfish feelings. But how can this be successfully accomplished, when the faculties and sentiments themselves, the laws to which they are subjected, and their relations to external objects, are unascertained? Accordingly, the theories and practices observed in education are innumerable and contradictory; which could not happen if men knew the constitution of the object which they were training.—*Geo. Combe.*

Nothing is comprehended so fully and distinctly, nothing retained so firmly, as that which we find ourselves. —*Kant.*

Each one of us has in himself his ideal prize man— that is, the harmonious maximum of all his individual predispositions; and it is the business of education to develop him into full growth.—*Richter.*

The educator must adapt himself to the pupil, but not to such a degree as to imply that the pupil is incapable of change, and he must also be sure that the pupil shall learn through his experience the independence of the object studied, which remains uninfluenced by his variable personal moods, and the adaptation on the teacher's part must never compromise this independence.—*Rosenkranz.*

The profession of pedagogy is the latest comer among the liberal professions of this country. The law, theology, and medicine, are already crowded so with partially and well-educated candidates, that the people are able to select the wheat from the chaff. No community of any considerable pretension is now compelled to take up with a pettifogger for its lawyer, a quack for its doctor, or an ignorant gospel ranter for its minister. The objective point of our system of Normal education is to stimulate the preparation of teachers, by agencies, public and private, popular and collegiate, till the same "glut in the market," enables the school committees to go into the field and choose the best the money supplied by the people will command.—*Rev. A. D. Mayo.*

The faithful and competent teacher never fails to secure the confidence, respect, and even affection of his pupils. He is, as he ought to be, esteemed "in place of a parent." He is thought to be infallible. He ought therefore, to be correct. He is esteemed as possessing the whole Cyclopædia of knowledge. He ought, therefore, to be a man of extensive acquaintance with the principles of science. He is thought by the confiding pupil to be incapable of any measure, or even intention at variance with honest views of promoting the best interests of those entrusted to his care. And he ought accordingly, to enlist all his energies in promoting the solid improvement and moral growth of every mind submitted to his influence.— *Wm. H. McGuffey.*

For precept must be upon precept, precept upon precept; line upon line, line upon line; here a little, and there a little.—*Isaiah.*

Learning is but an adjunct to ourself.—*Shakespeare.*

A mother tells her infant that two and two make four, the child is able to count four for all the purposes of life, till the course of his education brings him among philosophers, who fright him from his former knowledge by telling him that four is a certain aggregate of units. —*Samuel Johnson.*

Books, schools, education, are the scaffolding by means of which God builds up the human soul.—*Humboldt.*

Delightful task! to rear the tender thought,
To teach the young idea how to shoot.
—*Thomson.*

What is defeat? Nothing but education—nothing

but the first step to something better.—*Wendell Phillipps.*

Country schools need the very best teachers, men and women of broad views and culture, of experience and knowledge of human nature, men and women fitted to be leaders in these little communities. I know of no position of more influence than that of a teacher in a country district where a healthy public sentiment prevails. If possessed of any qualifications for leadership, the teacher becomes almost inevitably, a leader of thought and opinion. His influence is not bounded by the school-room walls, but extends to every home in the district. If this teacher be vain, frivolous, silly: if immoral or the slave of filthy habits, from that school will proceed influences that will curse every home in the district; if that teacher be pure, noble-minded, strong-souled, as a teacher ought to be, the streams flowing from that school will be streams of blessing, like those "which make glad the city of God."—*Mary Allen West.*

Now, I believe that a school, in order to be a good one, should be one that will fit men and women, in the best way, for the humble positions that the great mass of them must necessarily occupy in life. It is not necessary that boys and girls be taught any less than they are taught now. They should receive more practical knowledge than they do now, without a doubt, and less of that which is simply ornamental; but they cannot know too much. I do not care how much knowledge a man may have acquired in school, that school has been a curse to him if its influence has been to make him unhappy in his place, and to fill him with futile ambitions.—*J. G. Holland.*

Knowledge which costs nothing, which is not born of the travail of the soul, is fleeting and unprofitable. Explain a point to a class, be it never so clearly; impart information even of the most interesting and valuable character; and, if it be not fastened in the mind of the pupil, be not digested and assimilated by a subsequent mental operation, it will soon pass away. Gradgrind may fill the little pitchers ranged before him to overflowing, but they will not hold water. Here is the great benefit of class-drill and reviews. They force the mind to appropriate knowledge, and so retain what else would be suffered to escape.—*J. Dorman Steele.*

Do not seek happiness in what is misnamed pleasure. Seek it rather in what is termed study. * * * Learn to make a right use of your eyes; the commonest things are worth looking at, even stones and weeds, and the most familiar animals. Read good books, not forgetting the best of all; there is more true philosophy in the Bible than in every work of every skeptic that ever wrote; and we would be all miserable creatures without it.—*Hugh Miller.*

He who would teach well and to advantage, must not only understand the subjects which he is to teach; he must know how to enable it to grasp the mental food offered; and he must be able to put that food into such a shape that it may be grasped by the learner.—*Anna C. Brackett.*

Beyond his judicious preference for his own well-approved, though unpretending weapons; beyond his modest, but self-respectful reliance upon his own self-developed powers; beyond his prompt, but unostentatious acceptance of the duty and the trial providentially imposed upon him; beyond that imperturbable coolness and calmness which stamped him every inch a man, as well as a hero;—beyond all this, let the true teacher discover, and ponder well, that lesson of simple unwavering faith in a divine guidance and support, which he, in his conflicts with ignorance and insubordination, needs not less than did David in his memorable combat with the giant of Gath; and may he, in his time of need, both seek and find that guidance and support, and through them, come oft conqueror indeed.—*Jewell.*

The human mind is the brightest display of the power and skill of the Infinite Mind with which we are acquainted. It is created and placed in this world to be educated for a higher state of existence. Here its faculties begin to unfold, and those mighty energies, which are to bear it forward to unending ages, begin to discover themselves. The *object* of training such a mind should be, to enable the soul to fulfill her duties well here, to stand on high vantage-ground when she leaves this cradle of her being, for an eternal existence beyond the grave.—*Rev. John Todd.*

Men have tried many things, but still they ask for stimulant—the stimulant in use requires the use of more. Men try to drown the floating dead of their own souls in the wine-cup, but the corpses will rise. We see their faces in the bubbles. The intoxication of drink sets the world whirling again, and the pulses playing music, and the thoughts galloping, but the fast clock runs down sooner, and the unnatural stimulation only leaves the house it fills with the wildest revelry—more silent, more sad, more deserted, more dead. There is only one stimulant that never fails, and yet never intoxicates—

Duty. Duty puts a blue sky over every man—up in his heart may be—into which the sky-lark, Happiness, always goes singing.—*Geo. D. Prentice.*

INDEX.

Agreeableness	13-29
Architecture, School	55
Animal Food	16
Appetite for Fiction	21
Authors	20
Attractive, Make the School-Room	203
Automatons, Teachers as	200
Advanced Geography	118-183
Advanced Arithmetic	99-195
Advanced Spelling	89
Advanced Reading	81
Apparatus	62
Alphabetic Method	71
Alphabet	74
Alphabet Blocks	74
Autocrat of the School-room	46
Application for School	29
Associations, Teacher's	31
Attendance, Irregular	111
Anatomy, Physiology and Hygiene	149
Acoustics	153
Algebra	155
Attention, Habits of	43
Arithmetic	99-195

Astronomy	155
Accent in Reading	82
Addition	100
Articulation	69-75
Abbreviations	89
Addressing Letters	95
Analysis	73-112
Benevolence	11
"Big Head"	29
Bargains with Directors	30
Bright Pupils	49
Black-board, Necessity of	61
Black-board, Recipe for Making	209-62
Books for the Teacher	205
Blocks	50
Boards of Education, Secure Aid of	34
Boards of Education, Teachers instruct	57
Buildings	56
Beginning, Make a Good	35
Business, Show that you Mean	38
Bigoted Teachers	13
Biography, Works of	21
Botany	22-160
Brain, Well-balanced	13
Boarding	15
Bathing	17
Borrow Books	208
Bones	150
Bills, Merchant's	107
Beginners, Teaching, to Read	70
Capital Letters, Use of	79
Construction of School-houses	55-61
Calisthenic Exercises	51
"Coming Man"	46
Contract with School Boards	30
Costume	25
Coercive Measures	48
Collect Specimens	22-159

Cheating 174
Companions, Politeness to . . . 177
Circulation 152
Colds 67
Constitution of U. S. should be read in Classes 87
Compass of the Voice 82
Carbonic Acid 64
Compound Numbers 105
Cancellation 109
Convection 66
Classes 35
College Education 19
Cultivation 39
Child, Mind of 45
Crime and Education 56
Character 9
Conscientiousness 12
Cheerfulness 11
Calibre, Mental 14
Cleanliness 17
Chemistry 22
Coffee 17
Culture 18
College Discipline 19
Conversation 29
Conducting Recitations 39
Criticisms 43
Charts for Reading 74
Charts for Penmanship . . . 210
Copy-books 211
Commissioner of Education, Reports of . 207
Chewing and Smoking 25
County Papers 200–87
Compositions 133
Dress 25
Democratic form of Government . . 46
Despotism 46
Discipline 44

"Do Right," the only rule necessary . 47
Dismissal 52
Directors 28
Defining 88
Drawing 50
Drawing Maps 187
Dictionary, Unabridged 204-62
Dickens 20
Dignity 180
Drills, Oral 100
Deception 173
Diet 16
Digestion 152
Division 102
Denominate Numbers 105
Dictation Exercises 91
Difficult Words 95
Direction, Idea of 187
Dates in History 144
Disposition, Cheerful 11
Detective, Teacher as a 11
Draughts 65
Delivery 76
Declaration of Independence read in Classes 87
Decimal Fractions 109
Exercise 15
Eyes 153
Encyclopedias 62
Etymology 205
Encouragement, Give Words of . . 201
Enthusiasm 44
Enrolling Names 38
Employment 48
Expression 10-43
Essays 209
Experiments 165
Economy 175
Exhibitions 64

Elocution	69
Eclectic Method	73
Emphasis in Reading	78
Examination	39
Excitation	39
Firmness	12
Frankness	11
Foppishness	25
Finger nails, Attention to	25
Feuds Among Families	20
Farmer	29
Force in School-Room	48
Force in Reading	82
Free School System	56
Furniture	62
Failures, Study Your Own	202
Flowers	204
Fortunes not Made by Teaching	211
First day of School	38
First Reader	75
Fourth Reader	80
Fiction	20
Foul Air	64
Factoring	108
Fractions	109
Fruits	16
Geography, Primary	186
Geography, Advanced	183
Geology	22, 164
Greek and Latin	18
Grammar	193
Grades	36
General Exercises	52
German boy	53
Government	44
Generosity	179
Globes	62
Games	16

General Reading	20
General Knowledge	22
Grasping Thought	83
Hypocrite	9-200
Hygiene	15
History, U. S.	189
Hobby-riding	202
Highest Reward, The Teacher's	211
Higher Mathematics	155
Herbarium	22
Habits of the Teacher	25
Health	15
Horseback Riding	16
Honesty	173
Honor	11
Irregular attendance	111
Instruction	39
Institutes, Teacher's	32
Institute, Smithsonian	207
Influence of the Teacher	27
Impression, Make a good	29, 38
Illiteracy in proportion to Expenditure	56
Independent spirit	53
Investigation	44
Industry	174
Impure language	180
Inflection in Reading	78-82
Interest	110
Kindness	11
Know Thyself	14
Knowledge, General	22
Labor, Manual	16
Language	77
Language Lessons	127
Lying	173
Loafing	20
Listener, Teacher should be a good	29
Local Reporter	209

Library for Teachers . . . 204
Library for Schools . . . 63
Location of School-houses . . . 58
Letters 136
Love of the Work . . . 11
Love for study, how to incite . . 44
Lectures 42
Leaves, Collection of . . . 160
Leaves, Outline of 161
Latitude and Longitude, How taught . 119–125
Latin and Greek 18
Morals and Manners . . . 169
Moral Qualifications 9
Mental Qualifications . . . 10
Mental Arithmetic 99
Moroseness 11
Map Drawing 187
Map Drills 116
Mischief 46
Mind of the Child . . . 45
Majority, Voice of 47
Misdirected funds . . . 57
Material for School-houses . . . 61
Mottoes 203
Meddling spirit 28
Magnetic force 201
Manual labor 16
Magazines 20
Muscles 151
Mathematics 155
Multiplication 101
Merchant's Bills 106
Model Recitations 183
Model Spelling Lesson . . . 89
Models for Parsing 140
Mensuration 110
Music 22
Noise 47–61

Names, Write on Blackboard . . 48
Newspaper 86-93
Normal Schools 19
Novels 21
Natural Science 159
Natural History . . . 169
Numeral Frame 62
Notation and Numeration . . 100
Natural Tone in Reading . . 76
Number, Idea of . . . 99
Neatness 25
Order 12
Oral drills 100
Obstinacy 13
Organizing 37
Optics 153
Orthography 88
Odd Moments 20
Philoprogenitiveness 11
Physical Qualifications........................ 14
Primary Geography............................186
Punctuation 68
Pestalozzi, Quotation from..................... 44
Papers, Reading in school hours................ 49
Printing Press................................. 97
Pastry... 16
Preparation for Work........................... 18
Profession of Teaching......................... 31
Page, David P., Quotation from................. 23
Personal Habits................................ 25
Programme...................................... 35
Penmanship....................................210
Punctuality.................................... 26
Politeness..................................... 26
Preliminary work............................... 34
Political...................................... 31
Parents.. 27
Painting 22

Plan of School-house........................... 95
Profanity 181
Pictures in the school-room 203
Physics 165
Physiology 149
Property, Protection of........................178
Play-grounds................................... 58
Promptness 176
Purity of Speech...............................180
Poetic License................................. 81
Poetic feet 81
Pause in Reading............................... 83
Pitch in Reading 82
Processes before Rules.........................103
Position in Reading............................ 76
Perception Cultivated 77
Phonic method 72
Pronunciation 93
Patrons.. 27
Percentage 110
Qualifications—Moral 9
     Mental 10
     Physical........................ 14
     Scientific and Literary.......... 18
Questions...................................... 40
Quantity in Reading 82
Quality in Reading 82
Quiet school 47
Responsibility................................. 27
Rhetoric.......................................129
Recipe for Blackboard 209
Reports by the Government......................207
Relation of Teacher to Parents................. 27
Relation of Teacher to Society 31
Relation of Teacher to Profession 31
Religious creed................................ 31
Religious man 10
Rest... 51

Ride no Hobbies 202
Rewards, Teacher's Highest...................211
Recreation.................................... 16
Recesses 37
Reviews....................................... 40
Recitations, Manner of Conducting 39
Recitations, Model...........................183
Reverence....................................179
Respiration - - - - - 152
Reading - - - - - 20, 68
Rate in Reading - - - - 83
Radiation of Heat - - - 66
Regular Meals - - - - 16
Rules - - - - - 47
Respect - - - - - 178
System - - - - - 26
Scientific and Literary Qualifications - - 18
Social Qualities - - - - 13
School-Room - - - - 203
School-houses, Construction of - - 55
School-houses, Location of - - - 58
School-houses, Plan of - - - 59
School-houses, Surroundings of - - 58
School-houses, Size of - - - 59
Statistics - - - - - 56
School Boards - - - - 28
Shrubbery - - - - - 59
Studiousness - - - - 27
Society, Teacher in Relation to - - 31
Sunday School - - - - 31
Submissiveness - - - - 53
Self-government - - - - 54
Spirit of the Teacher - - - - 23
Spencer, Herbert, Quotations from - 53
Stories - - - - - 52, 86
Small pupils - - - - 52
Sympathy for pupils - - - - 201, 12
Slates - - - - - 49

INDEX. 241

Study, Time for - - - - 36
Swearing - - - - - 181
Skin, Health of - - - - 17
Stepping-stone, Teaching a - - 24
Scrap-book - - - - 42
Spelling - - - - - 88
Spelling Matches - - - - 91
Syntax - - - - - 133
Study your own Failures - - - 202
Strangers, Politeness to - - - 177
Speech, Purity of - - - - 180
Special Senses - - - - 153
Specimens, Make Collection of - - 159
Specimens to illustrate Physiology and Anatomy 154
Stress in Reading - - - - 88
Slur in Reading - - - - 88
Second Reader - - - - 77
Stoves - - - - - - 66–137
Subtraction - - - - - 101
Separatrix, Importance of - - - 105
Sentence writing - - - - 134
Student's Manual - - - - 206
Self-reliance - - - - - 12
Teaching Power - - - - 42
Teaching, Unconscious - - - 199
Teacher, Responsibilities of - - - 27
Teacher, Health of - - - - 14
Teacher, Qualifications of - - - 10
Teacher, In Relation to patrons - - 27
Teacher, In Relation to Society - - 31
Teacher, In Relation to Profession - 31
Teacher, Library of - - - - 204
Teacher, Spirit of - - - - 23
Teacher, Habits of - - - - 25
Talking too much - - - - 42
Topics - - - - - 40
Topic list for study of Geography - 118
Temperance - - - - - 16

242 INDEX.

Tobacco	17–25
Telephone	201
Tact	28–30
Taxation for schools	56
Tattling	173
Third Reader	78
Tables	107
Technical Grammar	128
Todd's Student's Manual	206
Tyrants	13
Tea	17
Teeth, Care of	25
Township Institutes	33
Unconscious Teaching	199
Unabridged Dictionary	204
Universities	170
U. S. Money	106
Unsuspicious	11
Vital processes	152
Venable's poem, Teacher's Dream	212
Variety in the school-room	51
Vegetables	16
Veracity	173
Ventilation	64
Visit parents	28
Visitors	51
Write Essays	209
Write for county papers, &c.	209
Written contract	30
Written Exercise	68–88–99–127
Wreaths as Decorations	203
Webster's Dictionary	204
Worcester's Dictionary	205
Wages	28–30
Whispering	48
Woods, Collection of	163
Wall Maps	62
Warming	66

Windows	61
Word Method	71
Writing Spelling	90
Words, Etymology of	205
Work, Preliminary	34
Webb Method	71
Weights and Measures	107

THE ONLY NORMAL PUBLICATION IN THE WORLD!

THE PRINCE OF SCHOOL JOURNALS!!

The Normal Teacher;

Acknowledged to be the most practical school periodical published. The only school journal in America that is the exponent of the Normal Idea of teaching.

It advocates those principles that are now revolutionizing the science and practice of teaching

It is not a literary magazine or a newspaper, like most of the school journals, but a periodical filled with practical hints and helps for the school-room, and devoted to the dissemination of Normal principles.

Its success so far has been unparalleled in the history of school journalism.

Remember that thousands of teachers and educators on both sides of the Atlantic have pronounced THE NORMAL TEACHER to be the most practical school journal published.

It regularly maintains the following special departments:

Grammar,
   Leading Articles,
      Notes and Queries,
         Correspondence,
            Editorial Notes,
               Examination,
                  College and Publisher's.

We give below a few of the many thousand opinions now on file at the office of publication:

"I am well pleased with Normal Teacher, and believe it a source of inestimable benefit to the cause of popular education. Hoping it may meet with unparalleled success in its grand mission, I shall do all in my power to aid its circulation among our teachers."—G. C. Gooper, Co. Supt., Dubois Co., Ind.

"I have been reading the Normal Teacher for more than a year, and consider it the most *practical* school journal I have ever seen. If our teachers want a *good* professional magazine, this will certainly suit them."—T. Bagot, Supt. Ripley Co., Ind. Schools.

"I like the Normal Teacher very much. I like its Western Americanism; its Scientific treatment of the School problem, of discipline, government, &c.; also, the Queries and Answers."—Prof. E. C. Cox, Stephenville, Texas.

"The Normal Teacher seems to be the only school periodical in America or in the world for ought I know, that grapples with the school problem as it is."—Prof. J. M. Long, A. M., Richmond, Mo.

"The Normal Teacher, published at Danville. Ind., is a monthly replete with most valuable information to teachers. Every teacher who wishes to keep posted in his profession, who would know how to discharge all the duties of the school-room, should read the Normal Teacher. It is one of the most popular and practical school journals published."—The Gongales,(Texas) Inquirer.

"From the hasty examination I have only been able to give the Normal Teacher I am deeply impressed with its value and marked merit. It must be of incalculable value to those for whom it is especially designed, and abounds in matter of great interest to educated people, whether teachers or otherwise."—S. N. Sanford, Pres. Cleveland Female Seminary, Cleveland, O.

Single subscriptions, - - - - - - - - - - - $1.00
In clubs of five and over, - - - - - - - - - - - .75

        J. E. SHERRILL, Editor and Publisher,
                            DANVILLE, IND.

PREPARE FOR EXAMINATIONS.

Special Announcement to the Teaching Profession.

THE NORMAL QUESTION BOOK;

Prepared expressly for the use of teachers in preparing for examinations.

Contains nearly four thousand questions and answers on the common school branches, arranged in a systematic and philosophical order. The Questions are such as to bring out the most difficult points in each subject and the Answers are taken from the best authorities, with the name of the author, the page, and paragraph from which each answer is taken.

The Questions and Answers are classified as follows:
Questions on Orthography.
Answers to Questions on Orthography.
Questions on Reading.
Answers to Questions on Reading.
Questions on Arithmetic.
Answers to Questions on Arithmetic.
Questions on Grammar.
Answers to Questions on Grammar.
Questions on U. S. History.
Answers to Questions on U. S. History.
Questions on Geography.
Answers to Questions on Geography.
Questions on Mathematical Geography.
Answers to Questions on Mathematical Geography.
Questions on Physical Geography.
Answers to Questions on Physical Geography.
Questions on Physiology.
Answers to Questions on Physiology.
Questions on Theory and Practice of Teaching.
Answers to Questions on Theory and Practice of Teaching.
Questions on Civil Government.
Answers to Questions on Civil Government.

The work was prepared expressly for the use of teachers in preparing for examinations; and is also adapted to the use of Common Schools, High Schools and Institutes for daily, weekly and monthly reviews. *With an Appendix*, containing outlines of Infinitives, Participles and Analysis in Grammar, Percentage in Arithmetic, Theory and Practice of Teaching, Map Drawing, A Scale of Criticism, A Programme of Studies and Recitations, Rules to be Observed During Examination, and Hints and Suggestions on the Preparation of Mss. Topic List for the Study of Geography, &c. By far the most complete and valuable work of the kind ever issued from the press.

An Immense Sale.

We believe that this book is destined to have a greater sale than any other School work yet published. The first edition and all but a few copies of the second edition were sold before a single copy of the book had been received from the hand of the printer.

Orders were received for it from nearly every State and Territory in the Union, from Canada and from England, previous to the day of publication.

Nicely and elegantly bound in cloth with gilt back and side-stamp printed in superb style on heavy white book paper and contains 406 pp. Price, *only* $1.50.

J. E. SHERRILL,
DANVILLE, Hendricks Co., Ind.

SOMETHING NEW.
Grammar Made Attractive and Interesting.
Wake Up Your Dull Grammar Class by Using
THE "NORMAL TEACHER" PARSING BOOK.

This little book contains forty-eight blank pages ruled and arranged for *written parsing lessons*, and several pages reading matter, consisting of programmes and models for parsing every part of speech, and for the analysis of sentences. Rules for distinguishing the different parts of speech in difficult cases, an explanation of the constructions of Infinitives and Participles and the Relative Pronoun. In short, a showing up, in convenient form, of the difficult points in Grammar besides the rules of Syntax, explanations and models for diagraming sentences, and other matter, all of which every teacher who knows anything about teaching Grammar will recognize at once as the most convenient thing imaginable to have in connection with the exercise book for use in the preparation of lessons. No one but the live teacher of Grammar knows the time and labor required in putting these forms and models on the board from day to day. The book is by no means a treatise on Grammar, but is simply matter arranged for the convenience of the pupil and to save the time of the teacher. Normal Teachers will want this little book in their schools at once and all who have had, or are having trouble in teaching Grammar would do well to adopt it also. It ought to be in use in every Grammar class in the land. WHY?

    1. Because by its use you can secure regularity and order in the preparation of parsing lessons and steer clear of the old haphazard, hit or miss style of recitation which makes Grammar "so dull and uninteresting."

    2. It cultivates systematic habits, is a drill in punctuation, penmanship and neatness, and gives pupils something to do.

    3. The use of written lessons gives great life and interest to the recitation through the comparisons, criticisms, &c.

    4. By having the exercises corrected each day where mistakes have been made, the pupil has his work preserved to him in permanent form, for future reference.

    5. Good teachers do not pretend to teach parsing, analysis, &c., in any other way than by the use of written lessons, to avoid waste of time, secure promptness and certainty of preparation. And all will prefer the Parsing Book from the fact that it is sold far cheaper than the blank paper can be bought at book stores. When these points are taken into consideration all must favor the immediate adoption of the book. Retail price, 20c per copy.

    Samples to teachers for examination, with a view to introduction into schools, 15c.

    Introductory rates by the quantity.: 6 copies for $1.00; 12 copies $1.75, 14 copies $2.00; 20 copies $2.25; 25 copies $2.50. Order at once. Address

    J. E. SHERRILL, Proprietor "Normal Teacher" Publishing House
                                                                    Danville, Ind.

(*IN PRESS.*)

NORMAL OUTLINES
OF THE
Common School Branches,

DESIGNED AS AN AID TO TEACHERS AND PUPILS IN THE METHOD OF TEACHING AND STUDYING BY TOPICS.

BY G. DALLAS LIND.

Author of Methods of Teaching in Country Schools.

PRICE, $1.00.

A VALUABLE BOOK FOR TEACHERS AND PUPILS.

Should be Introduced into Every School in the Land.

The Topic Method of instruction is fast coming into general use. The "old rote plan" is dying out. The text-book which is made up of questions and answers, and the teacher who merely asks these questions and expects the pupils to answer them in the language of the book, are both to be left far behind in this age of progress. It is the true province of the teacher to direct and infuse life and enthusiasm into the recitations, and the province of the pupil to investigate books and nature, and be able to give, in his own language, a full and correct report of his investigations. The pupil, thus, during the time of recitation, takes the place of teacher, and by teaching he fixes what he has learned by study.

This principle in teaching is as old as Socrates, for it was the plan he pursued. Jacotot and Montaigne, educators who lived in the days of Queen Elizabeth, strongly advocated this principle in teaching, and all the prominent educators from that time to the present have practiced it, but strange to say, the great majority of teachers still pursue a dead, dull routine of hearing pupils recite answers which they have committed to memory, or spend the time in lecturing to pupils while the latter merely listen and praise the wonderful genius of the teacher

This little book is designed to lift pupils and teachers out of these ruts by directing the studies of the pupils and stimulating them to investigation, and pointing out to the teacher the true plan of conducting a recitation.

The book contains an outline of a lesson for each day of a three month's term in each of the following branches, viz: Arithmetic, Geography, Grammar, United States History and Physiology, to which is added a list of examples for drill in the principles of Elocution, arranged under appropriate heads, and a list of test words in Spelling, and other miscellaneous matter of value.

In connection with the outlines are given references to the best text-books in use and also to many larger works on the subjects and to many works of a miscellaneous nature, which are found in libraries, both public and private. This is one of the valuable features of the work. It will lead the pupil out into the living pastures of knowledge and stimulate within him a desire to search further for truth.

By the use of this book different members of the class may have different authors. *No need of a uniformity in text-books except in Readers.* Correspondence solicited. Address

J. E. SHERRILL,
Danville, Indiana.

www.ingramcontent.com/pod-product-compliance
Lightning Source LLC
Chambersburg PA
CBHW031731230426

43669CB00007B/323